Jann Huizenga and Linda Huizenga

TOTALLY TRUE

Building Vocabulary Through Reading

OXFORD

UNIVERSITY PRESS

OXFORD
UNIVERSITY PRESS

198 Madison Avenue
New York, NY 10016 USA

Great Clarendon Street, Oxford OX2 6DP UK

Oxford University Press is a department of the University of Oxford.
It furthers the University's objective of excellence in research, scholarship,
and education by publishing worldwide in

Oxford New York

Auckland Cape Town Dar es Salaam Hong Kong Karachi
Kuala Lumpur Madrid Melbourne Mexico City Nairobi
New Delhi Shanghai Taipei Toronto

With offices in

Argentina Austria Brazil Chile Czech Republic France Greece
Guatemala Hungary Italy Japan Poland Portugal Singapore
South Korea Switzerland Thailand Turkey Ukraine Vietnam

OXFORD and OXFORD ENGLISH are registered trademarks of
Oxford University Press.

© Oxford University Press 2005
Database right Oxford University Press (maker)

Library of Congress Cataloging-in-Publication Data

Huizenga, Jann.
    Totally true : building vocabulary through reading. Book 3 / Jann
Huizenga, Linda Huizenga.
    p. cm.
    Includes index.
    ISBN-13: 978-0-19-430203-6
    ISBN-10: 0-19-430205-9
    1. Vocabulary—Problems, exercises, etc. 2. English language—
Textbooks for foreign speakers. I. Huizenga, Linda. II. Title.

PE1449.H83 2005
428.2'4-dc22
                                                        2004059973

Executive Publisher: Nancy Leonhardt
Senior Editor: Chris Balderston
Editor: Patricia O'Neill
Associate Editor: Amy E. Hawley
Assistant Editor: Hannah Ryu
Art Director: Lynn Luchetti
Design Project Manager: Amelia Carling
Designer: Michael Steinhofer
Layout Artist: Julie Macus
Senior Art Editor: Jodi Waxman
Production Manager: Shanta Persaud
Production Controller: Zainaltu Jawat Ali

ISBN-13: 978 0 19 430203 6
ISBN-10: 0 19 430205 9

Printed in China

10 9 8 7 6 5 4 3 2 1

ACKNOWLEDGMENTS

Cover photographs: Sunset: © Fogstock/Alamy; Skydiver: © Buzz Pictures/Alamy;
Surfer: © Buzz Pictures/Alamy; Taipei 101: © Associated Press.

Illustrations by: Art and Science, Inc. pp.36, 64; Adrian Barclay pp.11, 23, 39, 44, 51,
54 (café), 59, 71, 80; Sandra Bruce pp.8, 16, 26 (Match the words), 32, 54 (Match the
words), 72, 82 (Match the words); Jun Park pp.4, 12, 20, 48, 68, 76; George
Thompson pp.7, 19, 26 (picnic), 31, 40, 43, 52, 67, 79; William Waitzman pp.3, 15,
24, 35, 47, 60, 63, 75, 82 (kitchen).

We would like to thank the following for their permission to reproduce photographs:
AP/Wide World Photos p.62; J. Brian Alker/Getty images p.81;
aophotography.com/Alamy p.84; Bettmann/CORBIS pp.13, 41, 65; © Rebecca
McAlpin Photography p.53; Marnie Burkhart/Masterfile p.25; CORBIS p.33; Jim
Cummins/Getty Images p.45; Julia Fishkin/Getty Images p.58; ForeheADs Ad
Agency p.46; Steven Holt/stockpix.com p.18; Didrik Johnck/CORBIS p.9; JP
News/FedEx Washington p.5; Keyfoto/Alamy p.61 (spray paint); Paul Kronenberg
p.6; Tim MacPherson/Getty Images p.28; Ryan McVay/Getty Images p.37; Zoran
Milich/Masterfile p.21; Aimee Morgana p.73; Frank Noelker/The Fauna
Foundation p.70; Photodisc pp.61 (scissors), 78; PictureQuest p.10; Aram
Radomski/berlintapete.de p.42; Reuters/Kin Chong p.17; Reuters/Stephen Hird
p.77; Reuters/Christopher Furlong p.38; Reuters/Shamil Zhumatov p.2; Miguel
Salmeron/Masterfile p.22; Science & Society Picture Library p.74; SK/CP Taiwan
Taipei p.14; Stockbyte pp.56, 66; Orban Thierry/CORBIS SYGMA p.50; Veer p.69;
Adrian Weinbrecht/Getty Images p.34; Rob Wray p.30.

Special thanks to: iHost (James Nelson photo).

Contents

Welcome to *Totally True*. Let's take a look at a unit.

1. **Read the story** asks you to predict what the story is about, read it, and get to know the New Words.

2. **Rate the story** asks about your interest in the story.

3. **Check your comprehension** asks how well you understand the story.

4. **Check your vocabulary** helps you practice the New Words by completing sentences about the story.

5. **Listen to the story** gives you the chance to hear the story as you look at the pictures.

6. **Retell the story** helps you practice retelling the story using the pictures.

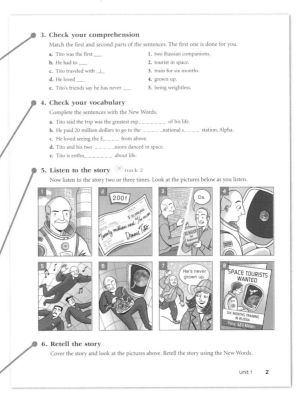

7. Answer the questions asks you to talk about the story and yourself.

8. Learn word partnerships builds on what you have learned by introducing words that go with one or two of the New Words.

9. Learn word groups builds on what you have learned by using pictures to introduce more vocabulary related to the New Words.

---

7. Answer the questions

About the story…
a. What did Tito have to do before going to space?
b. What did he like about his trip?
c. What kind of man is Tito?
d. What question would you like to ask him?

About you…
e. Would you like to go to space? Why or why not?
f. What is the greatest experience of your life?
g. Where do you most want to go sightseeing?
h. Who would you like to take as a companion?

8. Learn word partnerships

Study the partnerships below. Complete the sentences so they are true for you.

ENTHUSIASTIC		
be enthusiastic	about something	**Tito is enthusiastic about life.**
		I'm really enthusiastic about the trip.
		She's enthusiastic about sports.
	about doing something	We're enthusiastic about learning Chinese.
		He's not enthusiastic about traveling.
		I'm enthusiastic about swimming.

a. I'm really enthusiastic about _____
b. I'm not enthusiastic _____
c. I _____ enthusiastic _____ studying.

9. Learn word groups

Complete the sentences so they are true. Use words from the pictures.

SPACE

star
sun
moon
rocket
planet
Earth

a. The Earth goes around the _____
b. The sun is a _____
c. People have traveled to the moon in a _____
d. The sun, the _____, and the stars are in space.
e. Mars is called "the red _____."

4   Unit 1

---

10. Take a dictation gives you practice listening to a summary of the story and writing down what you hear.

11. Complete the story gives you a second story to review the New Words and other new vocabulary.

Talk about the stories gives you the chance to talk more about both stories.

---

10. Take a dictation 🔊 track 3

Use your own paper to write the dictation. Check your answers on page 86.

11. Complete the story

Use the words from the box to complete the story.

trips   space   international   planet
unbelievable   completely   train   rockets

The Wonderful Future of Flying

MIAMI, USA People have been flying for 100 years. What will the next 100 be like? NASA scientists* think they will be (1) _____ —a real golden age** for flying!

Big planes will get bigger, carrying up to 1,000 passengers on (2) _____ trips. At the same time, people will get their own small flying machines for shorter (3) _____. These machines will be easy to fly, so people will only have to (4) _____ for five days to get a license***. And they won't cost much more than a car. There may soon be one in every garage!

By 2025, says one scientist, it will be common for tourists to go into (5) _____. The price will drop to one million dollars. Jim Dator of the University of Hawaii says some people will go into space and stay there. "We may go to Mars for years," says Dator. "Because the (6) _____ is so far away," he says, "people will not travel back and forth.

(7) _____ will take groups of people to Mars, where they will stay, changing into a/an (8) _____ different kind of people."

* NASA scientists: people who study space
** golden age: very good and successful years
***license: a piece of paper that shows you may drive

🔊 **Talk about the stories**

What new things did you learn about space travel in this unit? Would you like to travel in space or live on Mars? Why or why not?

Dear Teachers,

Welcome to *Totally True*! If you are looking for an enjoyable and motivating way to help build your students' vocabulary, you've come to the right place. Vocabulary learning doesn't have to be difficult and dull. The goal of *Totally True* Book 3 is to make it fun. It teaches common words in the context of amazing true stories at a pre-intermediate level. The book is intended for classroom use, but it will also work well for self-study with the audio CD.

Totally True was written with two things in mind: 1) that everyone loves a great story and 2) that students acquire new vocabulary more readily when they meet it in engaging contexts and then use it in purposeful follow-up activities.

Research on vocabulary acquisition shows that most learning takes place when students meet new words in context, not in isolation. The content must be rich and interesting, and—even more importantly—understandable. The stories in *Totally True* satisfy these conditions: they are intrinsically entertaining while the accompanying pictures make them easy to understand.

The research suggests that context alone, however, is not enough for many students to learn new vocabulary. Formal, explicit instruction can help. Thus *Totally True* highlights new vocabulary in the opening stories and helps students to focus on this vocabulary in varied activities throughout the rest of each unit.

How can we make sure that new vocabulary will remain in students' long-term memories? At least two things are necessary: First, students need to process the vocabulary at a deep level—that is, they need to produce it. *Totally True* provides many opportunities for students to use the new vocabulary items in both speaking and writing, in meaningful and personalized ways. Second, students need multiple meaningful exposures to the vocabulary (as many as 7–12 times, some experts say). *Totally True* provides careful recycling—students revisit each new vocabulary item several times within each unit, as well as in the review units, and to some extent from unit to unit. The index on pages 97–99 shows where the vocabulary items are recycled. *Totally True* thoroughly integrates the four strands of listening, reading, speaking, and writing, and its activities are sequenced so that work on receptive skills precedes production. The book can be successfully used for general language acquisition or reading instruction as well as for the specific mastery of vocabulary.

We encourage you to adapt the material to suit the needs of your classes. We really hope you enjoy using the book, and we wish you every success.

Jann Huizenga

Linda Huizenga

Totally *Bookworms* Compatible

A key benefit of *Totally True* is that its language levels are tied to the *Oxford Bookworms* syllabus, so the series can be used together with *Bookworms* graded readers. The stories in *Totally True* Book 3 use the core structures and the vocabulary from *Bookworms* Stage 3. However, each opening story introduces 10–14 words above Stage 3. These words are highlighted in the story and treated as "New Words." Meeting these higher-level New Words initially in the rich context of a story helps students to understand them. Students continue to meet and produce the New Words in the activities throughout the unit, ensuring that these words become part of students' active vocabulary. Studying with *Totally True* Book 3 will help prepare students to move up to *Bookworms* Stage 4. *Totally True* can also complement any other extensive reading program. The stories and carefully designed practice activities will provide variety in teaching reading.

Level	Vocabulary	Core structures include:	Examples from *Totally True*
Oxford Bookworms Stage 1 and *Totally True* Book 1	400 headwords	simple present present continuous simple past	The boy does not like to be away from his **favorite** friend. Once the family took a trip, but they did not stay away long. "My son **missed** Lucky," said his mother. "So we came back early." *Python Boy* (Unit 2)
Oxford Bookworms Stage 2 and *Totally True* Book 2	700 headwords	present perfect *will* (future) *have to / must not could*	The city has given free books to subway riders **since** 2004, and wants to give away millions more in the future. The city hopes that readers will **return** the books when they finish, but no one is checking. *Fighting Crime with Books* (Unit 13)
Oxford Bookworms Stage 3 and *Totally True* Book 3	1,000 headwords	present perfect continuous past perfect *used to*	**Meanwhile**, their dinner was still cooking on the **stove** in the kitchen. They had completely forgotten about it! It started to burn, and the **flames** jumped quickly around the kitchen. The whole room and a nearby hallway were completely destroyed. *Cat and Couple Are Homeless* (Unit 13)

1. Read the story

Purpose: To engage students' attention, to train them to use prediction as a pre-reading strategy, to develop general reading comprehension skills, and to introduce the New Words in context.

Procedure: Before students read, ask them to cover the story and look at the pictures on the opposite page. As students make predictions about the story, help them with the vocabulary they need—especially key words and New Words from the story. If students call out words or phrases in their native language, translate them into English and write them on the board. Then ask students to read the story silently to see if their predictions are correct. Tell them to make their best guess about the meanings of the New Words—the words in bold. Tell students the numbered sentences in the story correspond to the numbered pictures. Within the context of the story and with the support of the pictures, students should be able to make good guesses.

After the first reading, students can check the meanings of the New Words in the glossary on pages 88–96. Encourage them to read the story again after this.

Alternative procedure: After students look at the pictures, ask them to write two or three questions they have about the story. Ask them to read the story to see if they can find answers to their questions.

2. Rate the story

Purpose: To encourage students to respond personally to the story and to develop critical reading and thinking skills, such as evaluating and giving opinions.

Procedure: After students mark an ✗ on the scale, ask them to share the reasons for their ratings with a partner or a small group.

Instead of having students do the "Rate the story" activity here, you could have them do it after activity 7. Alternatively, they could rate the story here and again after activity 7 to see if their opinions have changed.

Alternative procedure: If you have a small class, hang five pieces of paper in different places on the wall of your classroom. Each paper shows a different number from 1 to 5. After students have marked an ✗ on the scale, ask them to stand up and walk to the number that shows how they rated the story. Ask them to speak to one member of their group to explain their opinion of the story. After a minute, ask a few volunteers to share what they heard with the whole class.

3. Check your comprehension

Purpose: To see how well students understand the general meaning of the story.

Procedure: Encourage students to complete this activity without looking back at the story. Then have students compare their answers with a partner or a small group. If the activity causes difficulty, have students read the story a second time and try the activity again.

4. Check your vocabulary

Purpose: To help students focus on the use and spelling of the New Words, a first step in making the New Words part of their active vocabulary.

Procedure: Encourage students to complete this activity without looking back at the story. Then have students check their answers against the story or compare them with a partner or small group.

Alternative procedure: If the activity causes difficulty, have students complete it while looking at the story.

5. Listen to the story

Purpose: To give students an opportunity to hear the story and the New Words, and to prepare them to retell the story.

Procedure: Ask students to look only at the numbered pictures (not at the story). Play the CD. Students will probably want to hear the story more than once. Afterward, to assess students' listening, read the story to students yourself, making some factual "mistakes." Tell students to clap when they hear a mistake and then see if anyone in the class can correct it.

If you don't have the CD, read the story to students yourself. Say the numbers as you read so that students can look at the relevant picture at the right time.

Alternative procedure: To reinforce the New Words, write them on the board and point to them as the CD is playing. This will be especially appreciated by your more visually-oriented students.

6. Retell the story

Purpose: To give students oral practice, with a combined focus on story retelling and additional practice of the New Words.

Procedure: Have students cover the story and look only at the pictures. Elicit the story orally from the whole class first. Encourage students to call out the ideas of the story in chronological order and to use the New Words, telling them to paraphrase. Then ask students to practice retelling the story in their own words with a partner.

Alternative procedure: Put students in small groups and have them retell the entire story together by taking turns contributing a sentence at a time.

7. Answer the questions

Purpose: To encourage students to discuss the story, to relate it to their personal lives, and to meet and use the New Words in meaningful and personalized contexts.

Procedure: Ask students one of the questions from this activity. Give them time to think about the answer and then have them discuss it with a partner or a small group. Ask a volunteer or two to report back to the whole class. Then ask another question.

Alternative procedure for "About the story": To make sure all your students are involved in this activity simultaneously, follow this procedure:

a. Put students in small groups. Four is the ideal number.
b. Give each student a number (from 1 to 4).
c. Ask one of the "About the story" questions.
d. Tell students to decide on the answer together in their groups.
e. After about a minute, call a number (1, 2, 3, or 4). Have students with that number stand up and report back on their group's answer.

Alternative procedure for "About you": To provide students with some writing practice, allow each student to choose the one question that most interests him/her. Give students a time limit of about five minutes to write their answers. Then have students share their answers with a small group.

8. Learn word partnerships

Purpose: To build on what students have learned by introducing key collocations for one or two of the New Words.

Procedure: Tell students that they are going to learn a little more about one or two of the New Words. Have students study the chart. Explain that the New Word(s) in black often occur(s) with the words in green. Tell students that when they meet any new vocabulary, they should look at the words that surround it because learning a new word together with its "word partners" will lead to fluency faster than learning a word in isolation. This technique will also make them more accurate users of the language. Have students complete the sentences individually, and then ask them to share their answers with a partner or a small group.

9. Learn word groups

Purpose: To build on what students have learned by introducing new vocabulary that is thematically related to one or more of the New Words.

Procedure: Students already know one or two of the New Words pictured here, but they may not know the other words that are thematically related to it/them. Pronounce the words and allow students to repeat them. Then have students complete the sentences and share their answers with a partner or a small group.

10. Take a dictation

Purpose: To assess if students can hear and write the New Words in a story summary.

Procedure: Play the dictation on the CD and ask students to write what they hear—there is a pause after each breath group so they have time to write.

Play the dictation again to allow students to check their answers. Students then correct their work or their partner's work by looking at pages 86–87. You could use this as a test and collect the dictations. **Alternative procedure:** Read the dictation yourself at normal speed. Students should not write at this stage. Then read it again, pausing after each breath group so that students have time to write. Read the dictation a third time, at near-normal speed, allowing students to check their answers. Students then correct their work or their partner's work by looking at pages 86–87. Again, you could use this as a test and collect the dictations.

11. Complete the story

Purpose: To give students an opportunity to review the New Words, and other vocabulary from the unit, in a new context, and to provide additional reading practice using a story that is thematically related to the first one.

Procedure: Encourage students to complete this story individually, and then have them check their answers with a partner or a small group. They could then practice reading the story to each other.

Alternative procedure: If you have more advanced students, have them cover the story and try to retell it in their own words, using the words in the box.

Talk about the stories

Purpose: To give students additional oral practice using the New Words in a less structured way, and to develop critical thinking skills such as evaluating, comparing, contrasting, and giving opinions.

Procedure: There are two types of "Talk about the stories": discussion questions and role plays. For the discussion questions, give students a bit of thinking time. Then have them discuss their ideas with a small group or you could conduct a whole-class discussion.

For the role plays, have students work with a partner. Give them a time limit of a few minutes for their "conversation." You may have brave volunteers who want to reenact their conversation for the whole class!

Web Searches

If your students want additional information about a story, have them do a Web search by inserting a name or a topic into a search engine. This could be done as classwork or homework. At the time of publication, most of the stories could be found on the Internet.

Audio CD

The CD contains recordings of the first stories in each unit and the dictations. These are read by native speakers and provide great listening models and variety in class. You may prefer to play the story for students in activity 1, changing the focus of the activity from reading comprehension to pronunciation.

Totally True Teacher's Resource Site

The Teacher's Resource Site has downloadable unit tests that review all the New Words from each unit and help teachers and students assess progress. Answer keys for these tests and for *Totally True* Book 3 are also available at www.oup.com/elt/teacher/totallytrue.

Acknowledgments

We would like to thank those folks who helped us find the great stories for this book—our generous and talented colleagues Won-Mi Jeong and Stella Chen, our brother Joel (with his piles of clippings), and Jann's stalwart husband Kim (who spent countless hours finding and critiquing stories and then figuring out how to illustrate them). Thanks also to our father, John, who never complained when his tidy kitchen was transformed into our temporary office during visits.

We are also grateful to all the teachers and students in Asia who have participated in Jann's recent workshops. Their creative ideas and enthusiasm helped shape this series. These people include the brilliant and hospitable teachers and students at De Lin Institute of Technology in Taipei—in particular Fanny Lai, Stella Chen, Felisa Li, Gloria Chen, and Shi-Tung Chuang; the unforgettable teachers from the Korean National University of Education— especially Won-Mi Jeong, Eun-Jeong Ji, Young-Chai Son, Hee-Jung Park, Sun-Mi Kim, Jin-a Choe, Young-Hee Moon, Hyo-Gyoung Lim, and Joo-In Chang; and all the dear colleagues from Kumamoto Prefecture in Japan—including Rika Muraoka, Naomi Osada, Masaya Shindate, Hideaki Kiya, and Yayoi Umeda. It was an honor to work with everyone.

We'd like to give a special, heartfelt thanks to Dorota Holownia and Candy Veas, whose creativity and high spirits, as well as their intellectual and moral support on this and other projects, are always treasured.

Colleagues and students in Sicily, where much of this book was written, have also played an important role in this work, and we thank them for their very special friendships: Anna Reitano, Mary Puccia, Simona Barone, Giovanna Battaglia, Davide Fiorito, Simona Gambino, Antonella Gulino, Francesca Flaccavento, Rosaria Leone, and Giovanna Vernuccio.

In addition, we'd like to thank the following OUP staff for their support and assistance in the development of *Totally True*: Janet Aitchison, Oliver Bayley, Nick Bullard, Julia Chang, Tina Chen, Steven Ferguson, Satoko Fukazawa, JJ Lee, Constance Mo, Paul Riley, Amany Sarkiz, Julie Till, and Ted Yoshioka.

Finally, the publisher and the authors would like to thank the following teachers whose comments, reviews, and assistance were instrumental in the development of *Totally True*: Young-sung Chueh, Kumiko Fushino, Paul Jen, Sue Kim, Yonghyun Kwon, Richard S. Lavin, Jong-Chul Seo, James Sims, Daniel Stewart, Ching-Yi Tien, Carol Vaughan, Lisa D. Vogt, Gerald Williams, and Mei-ling Wu.

1

Space Tourist

1. Read the story

Look at the pictures on these pages.
What is the story about? Now read it.

LOS ANGELES, USA **1**"It was the greatest **experience** of my life," says Dennis Tito, 60, the first tourist in **space**. **2**In 2001, Tito, a California business person who has always wanted to be an astronaut*, bought a 20-million-dollar ticket to the **international** space station, Alpha.

3Tito had to **train** for six months and study Russian before traveling to space with two Russian astronauts. **4**He spent almost a week in space. "It was just **unbelievable**," he says, "to see the **Earth** from above and the black sky. It was like having a **completely** new life." **5**He loved being **weightless**

and dancing to Beatles music with his Russian **companions**. **6**He was always hungry for Italian food and enjoyed eating spaghetti in space.

7Tito's friends say he is **enthusiastic** about life, like a child. "He's never **grown up**," one said. **8**Now the Russian space program is looking for more space tourists like Tito. Would you like to go **sightseeing** in space? All you need for the **trip** is a strong interest, six months to train, and 20 million dollars!

_____

* astronaut: a person who travels into space

NEW WORDS

experience *n*	train *v*	completely *adv*	enthusiastic *adj*	trip *n*
space *n*	unbelievable *adj*	weightless *adj*	grow up *v*	
international *adj*	Earth *n*	companion *n*	sightseeing *n*	

>> See Glossary on page 88. >>

2. Rate the story

How much did you like it? Mark an ✗.

Not at All   A Lot
① ② ③ ④ ⑤

3. Check your comprehension

Match the first and second parts of the sentences. The first one is done for you.

a. Tito was the first ___   1. two Russian companions.

b. He had to ___   2. tourist in space.

c. Tito traveled with _1_   3. train for six months.

d. He loved ___   4. grown up.

e. Tito's friends say he has never ___   5. being weightless.

4. Check your vocabulary

Complete the sentences with the New Words.

a. Tito said the trip was the greatest exp_ _ _ _ _ _ _ of his life.

b. He paid 20 million dollars to go to the _ _ _ _ _national s_ _ _ _ station, Alpha.

c. He loved seeing the E_ _ _ _ from above.

d. Tito and his two _ _ _ _ _nions danced in space.

e. Tito is enthu_ _ _ _ _ _ _ about life.

5. Listen to the story   track 2

Now listen to the story two or three times. Look at the pictures below as you listen.

6. Retell the story

Cover the story and look at the pictures above. Retell the story using the New Words.

7. Answer the questions

About the story...

a. What did Tito have to do before going to space?

b. What did he like about his trip?

c. What kind of man is Tito?

d. What question would you like to ask him?

About you...

e. Would you like to go to space? Why or why not?

f. What is the greatest experience of your life?

g. Where do you most want to go sightseeing?

h. Who would you like to take as a companion?

8. Learn word partnerships

Study the partnerships below. Complete the sentences so they are true for you.

ENTHUSIASTIC		
be enthusiastic	about something	**Tito is enthusiastic about life.** *I'm really enthusiastic about the trip.* *She's enthusiastic about sports.*
	about doing something	*We're enthusiastic about learning Chinese.* *He's not enthusiastic about traveling.* *I'm enthusiastic about swimming.*

a. I'm really enthusiastic about _____.

b. I'm not enthusiastic _____.

c. I _____ enthusiastic _____ studying _____.

9. Learn word groups

Complete the sentences so they are true. Use words from the pictures.

SPACE

star

sun

moon

Earth

planet

rocket

a. The Earth goes around the _____.

b. The sun is a _____.

c. People have traveled to the moon in a _____.

d. The sun, the _____, and the stars are in space.

e. Mars is called "the red _____."

10. Take a dictation   track 3

Use your own paper to write the dictation. Check your answers on page 86.

11. Complete the story

Use the words from the box to complete the story.

trips	space	international	planet
unbelievable	completely	train	rockets

The Wonderful Future of Flying

MIAMI, USA People have been flying for 100 years. What will the next 100 be like? NASA scientists* think they will be **(1)** _____ —a real golden age** for flying!

Big planes will get bigger, carrying up to 1,000 passengers on **(2)** _____ trips. At the same time, people will get their own small flying machines for shorter **(3)** _____. These machines will be easy to fly, so people will only have to **(4)** _____ for five days to get a license***. And they won't cost much more than a car. There may soon be one in every garage!

By 2025, says one scientist, it will be common for tourists to go into **(5)** _____. The price will drop to one million dollars. Jim Dator of the University of Hawaii says some people will go into space and stay there. "We may go to Mars for years," says Dator. "Because the **(6)** _____ is so far away," he says, "people will not travel back and forth. **(7)** _____ will take groups of people to Mars, where they will stay, changing into a/an **(8)** _____ different kind of people."

* NASA scientists: people who study space
** golden age: very good and successful years
*** license: a piece of paper that shows you may drive

  Talk about the stories

What new things did you learn about space travel in this unit? Would you like to travel in space or live on Mars? Why or why not?

2

An Extraordinary Woman

1. Read the story

Look at the pictures on these pages. What is the story about? Now read it.

LHASA, TIBET ¹Sabriye Tenberken, 33, is an extraordinary woman with a big dream. She runs a school for **blind** children in Tibet and plans to open many more around the world. ²Sabriye is blind herself. Born in Germany, she lost her **sight** at age 13. ³But she made a **decision** to live life fully. As a **teenager**, she learned to ride horses, ski*, and go white-water rafting**. Nothing stopped her. Nothing frightened her.

⁴At **college**, Sabriye studied the **history** of Tibet. Afterward, she packed her suitcase, took her white cane***, and flew off to Tibet. ⁵There she bought a horse. With a **guide**, she rode along mountain **cliffs** to **distant** villages, looking for blind children for her school. ⁶She found many who were **desperate** to study.

⁷She teaches her students that they can do anything. They recently went white-water rafting and will soon **attempt** to climb one of Tibet's high mountains. ⁸Sabriye **believes** everyone has special **gifts**. Blind children, she says, will never be able to drive. "But they can read and write in the dark. And who can do that?"

---

* ski: to move over snow on long thin pieces of plastic
** go white-water rafting: to take a boat on a fast river
*** cane: a stick that is used to help people walk

NEW WORDS

blind *adj*	**decision** *n*	**college** *n*	**guide** *n*	**distant** *adj*	**attempt** *v*	**gift** *n*
sight *n*	**teenager** *n*	**history** *n*	**cliff** *n*	**desperate** *adj*	**believe** *v*	

>> See Glossary on page 88. >>

2. Rate the story

How much did you like it? Mark an ✗.

Not at All   A Lot
① ② ③ ④ ⑤

3. Check your comprehension

Put the sentences in the correct order. Number them 1–6. The first one is done for you.

a. ___ She learned to ride horses and ski as a teenager.

b. ___ She rode her horse, looking for children for her school.

c. ___ She studied the history of Tibet at college.

d. _1_ Sabriye became blind at 13.

e. ___ She bought a horse.

f. ___ She flew off to Tibet.

4. Check your vocabulary

Complete the sentences with the New Words.

a. Sabriye lost her si_ _ _ at age 13.

b. In Tibet, she rode a horse along mountain _ _ _ffs to find bl_ _ _ children.

c. She found children in dis_ _ _ _ villages who were _ _ _perate to study.

d. Sabriye _ _ _ieves that everyone has special _ _ _ts.

5. Listen to the story track 4

Now listen to the story two or three times. Look at the pictures below as you listen.

6. Retell the story

Cover the story and look at the pictures above. Retell the story using the New Words.

7. Answer the questions

About the story…

a. What kind of teenager was Sabriye?

b. Why did she go to Tibet?

c. What does Sabriye tell her students?

d. What do you think of her?

About you…

e. What is your dream for the future?

f. What are your special gifts?

g. What sports do you play?

h. What difficult thing do you want to attempt in the future?

8. Learn word partnerships

Study the partnerships below. Complete the sentences so they are true for you.

DECISION		
make a **decision**	to do something	***Sabriye made a decision to live life fully.*** *I made a decision to get a job.*
	about something	*I will have to make a decision about college.* *We made a decision about our future.*
an easy a difficult	decision	*I made an easy decision.* *It was a difficult decision.*

a. Last year I made a decision to _____.

b. When I get older, I will have to _____ a decision about _____.

c. I _____ a/an _____ decision today about _____.

9. Learn word groups

Complete the sentences so they are true for you. Use words from the pictures.

OUTDOOR ACTIVITIES

snowboard   skydive   hike   ride a horse   rock climb   water-ski

a. I love to _____.

b. In the future, I'd like to _____.

c. I don't want to _____ because I'm afraid.

10. Take a dictation 🔘 track 5

Use your own paper to write the dictation. Check your answers on page 86.

11. Complete the story

Use the words from the box to complete the story.

teenager	believe	blind	guide	distant	desperate	sight	skydive

Climbing Everest Blind

NEPAL   Erik Weihenmayer made history in 2001 when he became the first **(1)** _____ person to climb to the top of Mount Everest, the highest mountain in the world. How did he do it? Erik followed the sound of bells ringing on the clothes of other climbers.

Erik lost his **(2)** _____ as a young **(3)** _____, and his world became dark. Soon afterward, Erik lost his mother in a car accident. He felt **(4)** _____. But when his father began to take him mountain climbing in **(5)** _____ parts of the world, Erik began to **(6)** _____ in himself again. He became happy. He learned to climb by holding the shoulder of a **(7)** _____ as they walked together. Erik also learned to ski, **(8)** _____, and bike.

What did Erik "see" while he was on top of Everest? "Peace, success, and wide-open space," he says. "Blindness takes things away, but it gives you other things, and those new things can be as good or even better."

Talk about the stories

How are the lives of Sabriye and Erik similar? How are they different?

3

Living Without E-mail

1. Read the story

Look at the pictures on these pages.
What is the story about? Now read it.

LANCASTER, PA., USA ¹They look like they have stepped out of a nineteenth-century picture. The men wear dark suits and wide hats. The women wear long dresses and never cut their hair. ²Who are these people? They are the Amish, a group that lives in the Pennsylvania **countryside** and 22 other **states**. ³Some Amish do not own automobiles, preferring instead to ride in **carriages**. ⁴They live without **electricity**, telephones, e-mail, watches, or even zippers*. In a high-tech** world where life is changing fast, the Amish live **simply**, trying to keep old **customs** and **avoid** modern life.

⁵Many Amish are farmers, but others are furniture makers, flower sellers, or **basket** makers. ⁶Some Amish only go to school for eight years. After that, they work on their family's farm until they marry. ⁷In their free time, the Amish like to **sew**, **bake**, and play sports. They also like traveling by bus, but not by plane.

⁸Amish life is not completely **frozen** in time, but the Amish **consider** a new idea carefully before accepting it. "Will it keep my family together," they ask, "and my life **simple**?"

---

* zippers: long metal or plastic things that you pull
  to open or close things like clothes and bags
** high-tech: using modern electronic machines

NEW WORDS

countryside *n*	carriage *n*	simply *adv*	avoid *v*	sew *v*	frozen *adj*	simple *adj*
state *n*	electricity *n*	custom *n*	basket *n*	bake *v*	consider *v*	

>> See Glossary on page 89. >>

2. Rate the story

How much did you like it? Mark an ✗.

Not at All   A Lot
①   ②   ③   ④   ⑤

3. Check your comprehension

Check (✔) the endings that are true. The first one is done for you.

a. The Amish live

___ in two US states.

✓ without electricity.

___ simple lives.

___ without customs.

b. The Amish like to

___ avoid modern life.

___ travel by plane.

___ consider new ideas carefully.

___ keep their families together.

4. Check your vocabulary

Complete the sentences with the New Words.

a. Many Amish ride in _ _ _ _iages instead of cars.

b. They try hard to keep their old cus_ _ _ _ and av_ _ _ modern life.

c. The Amish often _ _k_ or s_ _ in their free time.

d. Before accepting new ideas, the Amish con_ _ _ _ _ them carefully.

5. Listen to the story track 6

Now listen to the story two or three times. Look at the pictures below as you listen.

6. Retell the story

Cover the story and look at the pictures above. Retell the story using the New Words.

7. Answer the questions

About the story…

a. Where do the Amish live?

b. What modern things don't the Amish use?

c. What jobs do they have?

d. Would you like to live as they do? Why or why not?

About you…

e. What technology do you use every day?

f. How long can you go without using a telephone?

g. What are two ways to make your life simpler?

h. What important customs are you attempting to keep?

8. Learn word partnerships

Study the partnerships below. Complete the sentences so they are true for you.

BAKE / SEW					
bake	bread		sew	a dress	
	cookies			a seam	
	a (chocolate/lemon) cake			a button on (a jacket, a shirt)	

Amish women like to bake bread and sew dresses.

I often bake cookies, but I never sew buttons on my clothes.

a. I'd like to try to bake _____.

b. My _____ bakes (a) wonderful _____.

c. I should _____ a button on my _____.

9. Learn word groups

Complete the sentences so they are true for you. Use words from the pictures.

CHORES

| bake | take out the garbage | do the laundry | wash the dishes | water the plants | sweep |

a. At home I often _____.

b. I don't like to _____.

c. My parents usually _____.

d. I should _____ more often.

10. Take a dictation track 7

Use your own paper to write the dictation. Check your answers on page 86.

11. Complete the story

Use the words from the box to complete the story.

bake	customs	simple	carriage	electricity	avoid	do the laundry

Traveling Back in Time

LONDON, ENGLAND   How long could you go without hot water, toothpaste*, or an indoor toilet? Could you live without your telephone and computer? A British TV show called *1900 House* asked those questions.

The show found a family that agreed to live a **(1)** _____ life for three months. The Bowler family traveled back in time to the year 1900. In their "time machine," they had to **(2)** _____ all modern conveniences**. There was no hot water, **(3)** _____, washing machine, TV, phone, or car.

The show was interesting to watch. The Bowler family arrived at the house in a **(4)** _____. For three months they followed all the old **(5)** _____ of 1900– wearing the clothes, eating the food, and even playing the games that were popular 100 years ago.

They quickly learned that the "simple" life was not easy! It was hard to **(6)** _____ bread. It was difficult to take a bath and **(7)** _____.

They always felt dirty. They often got angry. "Living in 1900 is not romantic***," Mrs. Bowler says. "It's dirty, hard work."

---

* toothpaste: what you put on your toothbrush to clean your teeth
** modern conveniences: machines that make life easier
*** romantic: about love

 ## Talk about the stories

How are the lives of the Amish and the Bowler family similar? How are they different? Would you like to live a simpler life? Why or why not?

4

A Moviemaker at Last

1. Read the story

Look at the pictures on these pages. What is the story about? Now read it.

TAIPEI, TAIWAN **¹**The international hit films* *Hulk*, *The Ice Storm*, and *Crouching*** *Tiger, Hidden Dragon**** have won hearts around the world. Did you know they were made by the same extraordinary man?

²Born in Taiwan, Ang Lee was **shy** and unhappy as a child. **³**He attended a high school where his father was the **principal**. As the oldest son, Lee had many **responsibilities** and was **expected** to do well at school. **⁴However**, he did poorly. "My head wasn't in the books," he says. When he failed the important college entrance **test** twice, his family was **disappointed** in him.

⁵In 1978, Lee went to the USA to become an actor, but his English wasn't good enough. **⁶**Then for 14 **tough** years he tried unsuccessfully to make a film. His pockets were empty, and he was desperate. **⁷**In 1992, Lee finally had some good luck. He won a **competition** in Taiwan to make a movie. He was a moviemaker at last! **⁸**These days, Lee's parents are **proud** of their Oscar-winning son, who makes hit films in Hollywood and Asia. "I can make movies **forever**," he says.

---

* hit films: movies that are very popular
** crouching: bending your knees and body so that you are close to the ground
*** dragon: a big animal with fire in its mouth; it is not a real animal

NEW WORDS

tiger *n*	**responsibility** *n*	**test** *n*	**competition** *n*
shy *adj*	**expect** *v*	**disappointed** *adj*	**proud** *adj*
principal *n*	**however** *conj*	**tough** *adj*	**forever** *adv*

>> See Glossary on page 89. >>

2. Rate the story

How much did you like it? Mark an ✗.

Not at All   A Lot
① ② ③ ④ ⑤

3. Check your comprehension

Correct five more mistakes in the story summary. The first one is done for you.

Ang Lee was a ~~happy~~ *shy* child. He attended a high school where his mother was the principal, and he did well there. When Lee went to the USA, he had four tough years. He tried unsuccessfully to make a film and became poor and desperate. But then he had some good luck. He won a competition in New York to make a movie. He was a moviemaker at last! Lee's parents are proud of their son, who makes hit movies in Hollywood and Africa.

4. Check your vocabulary

Complete the sentences with the New Words.

a. Ang Lee was a s_ _ child.

b. Lee was ex_ _ _ _ed to do well at school; how_ _ _ _, he did poorly.

c. When he failed the college entrance _ _ s _ twice, his family was _ _ _ _ppointed in him.

d. Lee says that he can make movies for_ _ _ _.

5. Listen to the story 🔘 track 8

Now listen to the story two or three times. Look at the pictures below as you listen.

6. Retell the story

Cover the story and look at the pictures above. Retell the story using the New Words.

7. Answer the questions

About the story…

a. Why was Ang Lee's life difficult as a child?

b. What happened when Lee went to the USA?

c. How did Lee's parents change?

d. What do you think is the most interesting thing about Ang Lee?

About you…

e. Have you seen any of Ang Lee's films? Which one is your favorite?

f. Would you like to be a moviemaker? Why or why not?

g. What responsibilities do you have?

h. How are you like Lee? How are you different from Lee?

8. Learn word partnerships

Study the partnerships below. Complete the sentences so they are true for you.

PROUD		
be proud	of something or someone	***Lee's parents are proud of their son.***
		My parents are proud of me because I work hard.
	of doing something	*She's proud of winning the game.*
		I'm proud of playing the piano.
	that + *clause*	*We're proud that we can speak English.*

a. I'm very proud of _____.

b. I'm proud that _____.

c. _____ is proud _____ me because _____.

9. Learn word groups

Complete the sentences so they are true. Use words from the pictures.

AT SCHOOL

 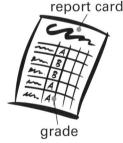   

score · test   report card · grade   diploma   book bag   locker

a. One hundred percent is a perfect _____.

b. Not many students like to take a _____.

c. I often put my books in a _____.

d. When you finish high school or college, you get a _____.

10. Take a dictation ⊙ track 9

Use your own paper to write the dictation. Check your answers on page 86.

11. Complete the story

Use the words from the box to complete the story.

tiger	expects	however	is proud of	forever	competitions

Action Queen

HONG KONG   Michelle Yeoh jumps from tall walls, flies through the air, and once even landed her bike on top of a fast-moving train. That's right! Michelle is an international action star* who does all her own stunts**.

The first time Michelle was in an action film, she had a quiet, calm part. She watched the men doing kung fu and karate and thought, "I can do that, too!" So Michelle studied martial arts*** 12 hours a day and kicked her way into a man's world. Since then, she has won many **(1)** _____. She has also made many movies. One of her most famous films is *Crouching* **(2)** _____, *Hidden Dragon*.

(3) _____, Michelle has paid a price for success. Her fights are real—and very dangerous. She has been burned and has hurt her legs, shoulders, and back. In her film *Ah Kam*, she had her worst accident, falling from a bridge and landing on her head. It almost killed her.

Michelle **(4)** _____ being an action star. She has started her own film company in Hong Kong and **(5)** _____ to continue in the film business **(6)** _____. "I love the excitement," she says.

---

   *action star: an actor who does dangerous things in movies
  **stunts: dangerous things that people do to amaze and surprise people
 ***martial arts: sports like karate and tae kwon do

 Talk about the stories

Which job is the most interesting to you—Ang Lee's or Michelle Yeoh's? Why?

5

Trash House

1. Read the story

Look at the pictures on these pages.
What is the story about? Now read it.

KINGMAN, ARIZ., USA [1]As the earth gets more crowded, the mountains of trash in every town and **city** are growing. What should we do with all this junk*? [2]Sharon and Jack Ehrhardt are helping to **solve** the problem. Their house is made of trash. They **collected** most of the **building materials** for the house themselves—for free! [3]The outside walls are made of about 1,000 used **tires** that were filled with **dirt** and then covered with plaster**. [4]The inside walls **consist of** old cans and glass bottles, which are covered with a coat of dirt and **mud**. [5]The thick walls make the home **extremely** strong. **Since** they move as the earth moves, the house can't be damaged in an **earthquake**.

[6]The **couple** gets electricity from the sun. They collect rainwater for taking baths and washing clothes and dishes. [7]The back of the house is **buried** under a small hill, which helps to keep it cool in the summer. [8]The Ehrhardts are **delighted** with their earth-friendly home, called an "Earthship." Earthships are becoming more and more popular with people who are tired of trash.

---

* junk: things that are not important or useful
** plaster: something that is used to cover walls; it becomes hard when it is dry

NEW WORDS

city *n*	building material *n*	consist of *v*	since *conj*	bury *v*
solve *v*	tire *n*	mud *n*	earthquake *n*	delighted *adj*
collect *v*	dirt *n*	extremely *adv*	couple *n*	

>> See Glossary on page 90. >>

2. Rate the story

How much did you like it? Mark an ✗.

Not at All   A Lot
①　②　③　④　⑤

3. Check your comprehension

Match the first and second parts of the sentences.

a. The Ehrhardts are helping to solve ___	**1.** old bottles and used tires.
b. They built their house with ___	**2.** the trash problem.
c. It is extremely strong and can't be damaged by ___	**3.** their Earthship.
d. The Ehrhardts get their electricity from ___	**4.** an earthquake.
e. The couple is delighted with ___	**5.** the sun.

4. Check your vocabulary

Complete the sentences with the New Words.

a. The Ehrhardts _ _ _lected most of the building _ _ _erials for their house.

b. The outside walls were made of old ti_ _ _ filled with d_ _ _.

c. The inside walls _ _ _sist of old cans and bottles.

d. An ear_ _ _ _ _ _ _ cannot damage an Earthship.

e. The back of the house is _ _ _ied under a hill.

5. Listen to the story track 10

Now listen to the story two or three times. Look at the pictures below as you listen.

6. Retell the story

Cover the story and look at the pictures above. Retell the story using the New Words.

7. Answer the questions

About the story…

a. What kind of materials did the Ehrhardts collect for their house?

b. Where do their electricity and water come from?

c. How do they feel about their home?

d. Would you like to live in an Earthship? Why or why not?

About you…

e. What do you do to help the earth?

f. How can you save electricity and water?

g. What are two other things you can do to save the earth?

h. Are you delighted with your home? Why or why not?

8. Learn word partnerships

Study the partnerships below. Complete the sentences so they are true for you.

DELIGHTED		
be delighted	with something	**The Ehrhardts are delighted with their Earthship.** *I'm delighted with my new computer.* *The teacher is delighted with the students' progress.*
	to do something	*I'm delighted to meet you!* *I'll be delighted to see my family again.*

a. I was delighted _____ meet _____.

b. I'm delighted _____ my new _____.

c. I'll be delighted to see _____.

9. Learn word groups

Answer the questions so they are true for you. Use words from the pictures.

BUILDING MATERIALS

stone

wood

tile

brick

a. What is your house or apartment made of?

_____

b. What is your desk made of?

_____

bamboo

c. Look around you. What building materials do you see?

_____

10. Take a dictation 🔘 track 11

Use your own paper to write the dictation. Check your answers on page 86.

11. Complete the story

Use the words from the box to complete the story.

bamboo	collect	city	extremely	is delighted with	solve

Trash Island

YUCATAN, MEXICO Do you ever worry about the mountains of bottles that we use every day? How can we **(1)** _____ the problem of too much trash?

A British man, Richard Sowa, was living near a beautiful beach in the Yucatan when he had an idea. He noticed some plastic bottles lying on the beach. "I'll use them to build myself a floating* island home!" he thought. Sowa asked friends, neighbors, and schoolchildren to help him **(2)** _____ empty bottles. It became a community project**. When they found 100,000 bottles, Sowa was ready to build his dream house.

He put all the plastic bottles into fishnets*** and tied them tightly. This became the bottom of his floating home. He used sand to make a floor and nearby **(3)** _____ plants to make his furniture. He even has a shower on his island, which floats just off the beach.

Sowa likes living far from the **(4)** _____, and he **(5)** _____ his earth-friendly home. "He's a dreamer," said his mother. "At first we thought he was crazy, but now we're **(6)** _____ proud of him."

* floating: staying on top of the water
** community project: work that neighbors do together
*** fishnets: things that are used to catch fish

Talk about the stories

Where would you rather live—in an Earthship or on a trash island? Why?

6

He Really Wanted to Survive

1. Read the story

Look at the pictures on these pages. What is the story about? Now read it.

ABERDEEN, WASH., USA **1**Jens Eventyr, 32, was alone in the Pacific **Ocean** one afternoon on his surfboard* when a storm came in. **2**The water turned **rough**, and strong **waves**, four meters high, pulled Jens away from the beach. **3**As the sun was going down, he saw a ship. "I screamed as loud as I could, but no one heard me," Jens said later. "It got dark, and I knew that the only one who could save me was me." **4**The **shore** became more and more distant.

5All night Jens **held on** to his surfboard. The water was icy cold, and it was raining hard. **6**Jens was **exhausted, weak,** and close to **drowning**. "It was **horrible**. I was at the edge of death the **whole** night. I wanted to fall asleep, but there was a voice telling me, 'Stay awake!'" **7**Just when Jens couldn't hold on **any longer**, the sun began to **rise**. **8**The wind changed, and he rode a big wave all the way to the beach. Jens was **fortunate**. "He really wanted to **survive**," said a police officer.

* surfboard: a long, plastic thing that people use to ride on waves in the ocean

NEW WORDS

ocean *n*	shore *n*	weak *adj*	whole *adj*	fortunate *adj*
rough *adj*	hold on *v*	drown *v*	any longer *adv*	survive *v*
wave *n*	exhausted *adj*	horrible *adj*	rise *v*	

>> See Glossary on page 90. >>

2. Rate the story

How much did you like it? Mark an **✗**.

Not at All   A Lot

①   ②   ③   ④   ⑤

3. Check your comprehension

Correct five mistakes in the story summary.

Jens Eventyr was alone in the Pacific Ocean on a surfboard when a storm came in. Some weak waves pulled him away from the beach, and the shore became more and more distant. Jens held on to his board the whole day. He almost drowned, but just when he thought he could not survive any longer, the moon began to rise. The wind changed, and he rode a wave to a ship. Jens was unlucky.

4. Check your vocabulary

Complete the sentences with the New Words.

a. Jens was alone in the Pacific O_ _ _ _ when the water turned ro_ _ _.

b. Jens h_ _ _ on to his surfboard as the sh_ _ _ became more distant.

c. He became exhau_ _ _ _ and w_ _ _.

d. "It was hor_ _ _ _ _," the fort_ _ _ _ _ man said later.

5. Listen to the story   track 12

Now listen to the story two or three times. Look at the pictures below as you listen.

6. Retell the story

Cover the story and look at the pictures above. Retell the story using the New Words.

7. Answer the questions

About the story...

a. What pulled Jens away from the beach?

b. What helped him survive the long night?

c. What happened when the sun rose?

d. What questions would you like to ask Jens?

About you...

e. How do you feel when you're at the beach?

f. Have you ever felt close to drowning? What did you do?

g. Do you think you could survive a night in the water? Why or why not?

h. What was a time in your life when you felt fortunate?

8. Learn word partnerships

Study the partnerships below. Complete the sentences so they are true for you.

SURVIVE		
survive	a horrible night	**Jens survived a horrible night in the ocean.**
	an earthquake	*I survived an earthquake two years ago.*
	a heart attack	*My uncle survived a heart attack in 2004.*
	a car accident	*We survived a bad car accident in Rome.*
	an illness	*Many people survive illnesses like cancer.*
	a typhoon	*Not everyone survived the typhoon.*

a. I survived _____ in _____.

b. My _____ survived _____ in _____.

c. I read in the newspaper about someone who survived _____.

9. Learn word groups

Answer the questions so they are true for you. Use words from the picture.

AT THE BEACH

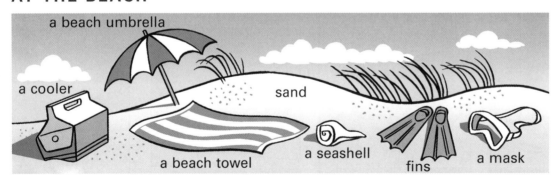

a. Think about a beach you visit. What can you find there? _____

b. What do you take to the beach? _____

c. What do you take home from the beach? _____

10. Take a dictation   track 13

Use your own paper to write the dictation. Check your answers on page 86.

11. Complete the story

Use the words from the box to complete the story.

| exhausted | waves | survived | whole | shores | fins | ocean |

70-YEAR-OLD SURVIVES 19 HOURS AT SEA

ISHIGAKI, JAPAN   An adventurous* Japanese man who wanted to try something new for his seventieth birthday was pulled out into the **(1)** _____ for 19 hours. Hideo Murasugi was snorkeling** for the first time in his life when strong **(2)** _____ pulled him away from the **(3)** _____ of Ishigaki Island in southern Japan. Murasugi was in the water for the **(4)** _____ night while he waited for the wind to change. His **(5)** _____ helped him stay above water. He knew he was not far from shore because he was still able to see lights.

Almost one day after entering the water, Murasugi swam back to the beach. He had **(6)** _____ the long night! He was **(7)** _____ and weak, but very fortunate. "It was my first time snorkeling, but I've had enough of it for a lifetime," he said.

---

* adventurous: liking new and exciting things
** snorkeling: swimming underwater with fins and a mask

 Talk about the stories

Imagine that you and a partner are Jens Eventyr and Hideo Murasugi. You are meeting for the first time. Tell your partner about your horrible night.

1. Match the words with the pictures.

___ **a.** city

___ **b.** tire

___ **c.** building materials

___ **d.** Earth

___ **e.** test

___ **f.** carriage

___ **g.** tiger

___ **h.** countryside

1.

2.

3.

4.

5.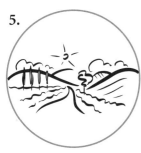

6.

7.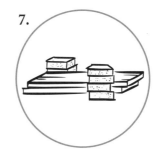

8.

2. Write the words in the picture.

| cliff | shore | ocean | wave | basket | couple |

3. Are the sentences true or false? Check (✓) the correct box.

	T	F
a. The sun rises in the evening.	☐	☐
b. You can drown in the ocean if you're not careful.	☐	☐
c. The opposite of "strong" is "weak."	☐	☐
d. A tiger is a small cat.	☐	☐
e. The USA consists of states.	☐	☐
f. Dirt is wet mud.	☐	☐
g. The opposite of "far" is "distant."	☐	☐

4. Cross out the item that *cannot* complete each sentence.

a. She studied _____.

    1. history   2. any longer   3. extremely hard   4. at college

b. They live near _____.

    1. the shore   2. the city   3. a cliff   4. an earthquake

c. She likes to _____ on weekends.

    1. take trips   2. sew   3. drown   4. go sightseeing

d. He has been sick for a week and feels _____.

    1. enthusiastic   2. exhausted   3. weak   4. horrible

5. Match the definitions with the words.

a. consider ___	1. to put something under the ground
b. blind ___	2. to think carefully about something
c. unbelievable ___	3. a choice that you make after thinking
d. bury ___	4. not calm or gentle
e. guide ___	5. very surprising or unusual
f. rough ___	6. not able to see
g. gift ___	7. without hope; ready to do anything to get what you want
h. decision ___	8. a person who shows people where to go
i. desperate ___	9. something you can do well or easily

6. Use the words from the box to complete the sentences.

fortunate	sight	international	whole	since	simply
teenager	customs	consist of	mud	weightless	expected

a. Dennis Tito loved being _____ in the _____ space station.

b. Sabriye Tenberken lost her _____ when she was a _____.

c. The Amish try to live _____ and keep their old _____.

d. Ang Lee was _____ to do well in school _____ he was the oldest son of a school principal.

e. The inside walls of the "trash house" _____ old cans, bottles, and _____.

f. Jens Eventyr was _____ to survive the _____ night in the ocean.

7. Use the words from the box to complete the story.

however	holding on	frozen
experience	tough	whole	distant

Man Can't Get Out of Tree

MANGALIA, ROMANIA

Catalin Pavel, 25, had a strange **(1)** _____ recently. He saw a cat that was high up in a tree and afraid to come down. So Pavel decided to climb up and get it. **(2)** _____, when he got up into the tree, Pavel was afraid to go down, just like the cat. He spent a **(3)** _____ day and night in the tree, **(4)** _____ tight.

Pavel shouted for help and finally, after a **(5)** _____ 24 hours, **(6)** _____

neighbors heard his calls. They called firemen, who helped Pavel and the cat get down. Pavel said that he was **(7)** _____ with fear after he got to the top of the tree and realized how high he was.

8. Check (✓) yes or no.

	Yes	No			Yes	No
a. I am shy.	☐	☐	**f.** I avoid red meat.		☐	☐
b. I am a principal.	☐	☐	**g.** I'm a teenager.		☐	☐
c. I like to take tests.	☐	☐	**h.** I'm attempting to learn English.		☐	☐
d. I love to bake.	☐	☐	**i.** I have responsibilities at home.		☐	☐
e. I'm good at solving problems.	☐	☐	**j.** I live a simple life.		☐	☐

9. Complete the sentences so they are true for you.

a. My favorite companions are _____.

b. I believe that _____.

c. I took a trip _____.

d. I am disappointed that _____.

e. I grew up in _____.

f. I'm training myself to _____.

g. I want to _____ forever.

h. I'm proud of _____.

10. Fill in the chart with names of classmates. Try to write a different name in each blank. Walk around the room and ask questions such as:

Do you like to swim in the ocean?
Do you feel completely exhausted?

The winner is the first person to fill in seven blanks.

FIND SOMEONE WHO...

a. likes to swim in the ocean. _____

b. feels completely exhausted. _____

c. has some international friends. _____

d. likes to sew. _____

e. avoids sugar. _____

f. would like to take a trip to space. _____

g. likes history. _____

h. is enthusiastic about school. _____

i. has a lot of responsibilities at home. _____

j. had an interesting experience last week. _____

7

Dream Jobs

1. Read the story

Look at the pictures on these pages.
What is the story about? Now read it.

CALIFORNIA, USA **¹**What is your dream job? **According to** recent surveys*, many British teenagers dream of working with computers. Japanese teens most often **mentioned** running a restaurant or being a **professor**.

²Some lucky Californians have found their dream jobs. Annie Lever is a **professional** dog walker. "I love my job," she says. Lever walks about 15 dogs a day in parks around Los Angeles, **earning** $25.00 a day for each dog. **³**She enjoys dogs, her **freedom**, and being outdoors.

⁴Andy Alamano, 24, is doing his dream job as a video-game **tester** for a company in San Francisco. His **hobby**—playing video games—has become his job! **At present** he earns $40,000 a year. **⁵**It is not all fun and games, **though**. "I have to sit through a lot of meetings**, too," says Alamano.

⁶When Wally Amos began baking cookies*** in Hollywood, his friends thought they were **delicious**. **⁷**So he went into business and was soon selling cookies around the world. "I love what I do," he says, "and I'm the **boss**." **⁸**Amos tells young people to keep their eyes open for a great job. "Listen! **Opportunity** is everywhere."

---

* surveys: questions that find out what people think
** meetings: times when people come together to talk
*** cookies: small, thin cakes

NEW WORDS

according to *prep*	**professional** *adj*	**tester** *n*	**though** *adv*	**opportunity** *n*
mention *v*	**earn** *v*	**hobby** *n*	**delicious** *adj*	
professor *n*	**freedom** *n*	**at present** *adv*	**boss** *n*	

>> See Glossary on page 91. >>

2. Rate the story

How much did you like it? Mark an ✗.

Not at All   A Lot
① ② ③ ④ ⑤

3. Check your comprehension

Correct five mistakes in the story summary.

Some lucky Californians have found their dream jobs. Annie Lever is a dog walker, earning $25.00 a week for each dog that she walks. She enjoys her freedom and being indoors. Andy Alamano is doing his dream job as a video-game tester. At present, he earns $40,000 a month. Wally Amos sells delicious cookies around the United States. He loves what he does. "Listen!" he tells young people. "Opportunity is nowhere."

4. Check your vocabulary

Complete the sentences with the New Words.

a. Acc_ _ _ _ _ _ to surveys, many Japanese teens dream of being a pr_ _ _ _ _ _ _ _.

b. Annie Lever, a pro_ _ _ _ _ _ _ _ _ dog walker, loves her fr_ _ _ _ _.

c. Andy Alamano _ _ _ _s $40,000 a year at pr_ _ _ _ _.

d. Wally Amos likes his job because he is his own b_ _ _.

5. Listen to the story   track 14

Now listen to the story two or three times. Look at the pictures below as you listen.

6. Retell the story

Cover the story and look at the pictures above. Retell the story using the New Words.

7. Answer the questions

About the story...

a. What does Annie Lever like about her job?

b. What does Andy Alamano do?

c. How much do Annie and Andy earn?

d. What does Wally Amos tell young people?

About you...

e. Which of the three jobs in the story looks the most interesting to you? Why?

f. Do you know people who have fun while working? What do they do?

g. Name two or three jobs that you would like.

h. What is your hobby?

8. Learn word partnerships

Study the partnerships below. Complete the sentences so they are true for you.

OPPORTUNITY		
a great a fantastic	opportunity	***Great opportunities are everywhere!*** *My trip to London was a fantastic opportunity.*
have the opportunity to do something		*I had the opportunity to meet my hero!* *He has the opportunity to travel for work.* *She hopes to have the opportunity to study.*

a. Last year I had an opportunity to _____.

b. My trip to _____ was a _____.

c. In the future I hope to _____ the opportunity to _____.

9. Learn word groups

Answer the questions so they are true for you. Use words from the pictures.

JOBS

a business person   a builder   a professional athlete   a judge   a fire fighter   a baker

a. Which of these jobs look boring? _____

b. Which job is the most difficult? _____

c. Which is the most dangerous? _____

d. Which is the most interesting to you? _____

10. Take a dictation track 15

Use your own paper to write the dictation. Check your answers on page 86.

11. Complete the story

Use the words from the box to complete the story.

earn	though	at present	boss
professional	according to	freedom	builder

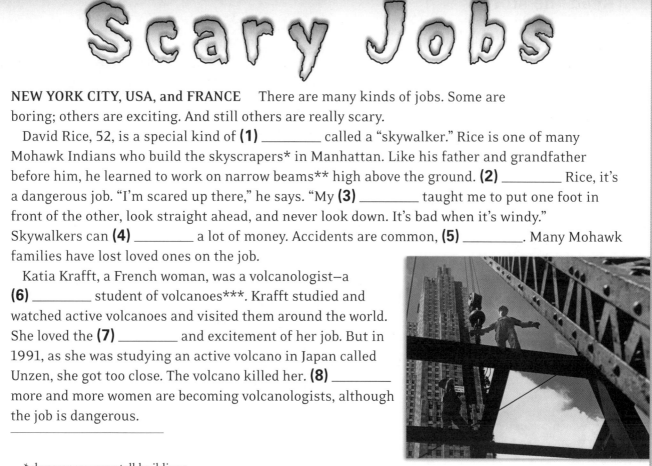

Scary Jobs

NEW YORK CITY, USA, and FRANCE   There are many kinds of jobs. Some are boring; others are exciting. And still others are really scary.

David Rice, 52, is a special kind of **(1)** _____ called a "skywalker." Rice is one of many Mohawk Indians who build the skyscrapers* in Manhattan. Like his father and grandfather before him, he learned to work on narrow beams** high above the ground. **(2)** _____ Rice, it's a dangerous job. "I'm scared up there," he says. "My **(3)** _____ taught me to put one foot in front of the other, look straight ahead, and never look down. It's bad when it's windy." Skywalkers can **(4)** _____ a lot of money. Accidents are common, **(5)** _____. Many Mohawk families have lost loved ones on the job.

Katia Krafft, a French woman, was a volcanologist—a **(6)** _____ student of volcanoes***. Krafft studied and watched active volcanoes and visited them around the world. She loved the **(7)** _____ and excitement of her job. But in 1991, as she was studying an active volcano in Japan called Unzen, she got too close. The volcano killed her. **(8)** _____ more and more women are becoming volcanologists, although the job is dangerous.

_____

* skyscrapers: very tall buildings
** beams: long, heavy pieces of wood that hold up a building
*** volcanoes: mountains with a hole in the top where fire sometimes comes out

 Talk about the stories

Which job from the two stories do you like best? Why? Which one don't you like? Why?

8

What Are Their Secrets?

1. Read the story

Look at the pictures on these pages.
What is the story about? Now read it.

OKINAWA, JAPAN **¹Imagine** a place where people are super-fit* and heart disease and cancer** are **rare**. It's not a dream! It's Okinawa, a Japanese island. Okinawans live longer than people anywhere **else** in the world.

²What are their secrets? Dr. Makoto Suzuki, who studied Okinawans for 25 years, wrote a book that explains their **habits**. ³The first key to their long lives is good eating. Most Okinawan elders*** eat **at least** seven fruits and vegetables a day. They **are fond of** fish and avoid red meat. They are also **regular** eaters of tofu. ⁴And they eat **light** meals, stopping before they're full. "Eat until you're 8/10 full," they say.

⁵Elders in Okinawa don't sit in front of the TV all day—they work in their gardens, dance, and do tai chi. **As a result**, their hearts and **bones** stay healthy. ⁶They live on "Okinawan time," enjoying life and never **rushing**. ⁷Elders also have extremely close **ties** to family and friends.

⁸Okinawans have 80 percent fewer **heart attacks** than Americans. Sadly, however, life on the island is changing. As fast-food restaurants and Western habits become more popular, lives are getting shorter.

---

* super-fit: very healthy
** cancer: a very serious illness that makes some cells (very small parts in the body) grow too fast
*** elders: people who are older than other people in the same group

NEW WORDS

imagine *v*	**habit** *n*	**regular** *adj*	**bone** *n*	**heart attack** *n*
rare *adj*	**at least** *adv*	**light** *adj*	**rush** *v*	
else *adv*	**be fond of** *v*	**as a result** *adv*	**tie** *n*	

>> See Glossary on page 91. >>

2. Rate the story

How much did you like it? Mark an ✗.

Not at All   A Lot

① ② ③ ④ ⑤

3. Check your comprehension

Check (✓) the endings that are true.

a. Okinawan elders live

___ on an island.

___ very long lives.

___ in front of their TVs.

___ on "Okinawan time."

___ rushed lives.

b. Okinawan elders eat

___ a lot of fish.

___ a lot of red meat.

___ tofu regularly.

___ heavy meals.

___ until they're completely full.

4. Check your vocabulary

Complete the sentences with the New Words.

a. Heart disease and heart _ _ _acks are r_ _ _ on Okinawa.

b. Okinawan elders eat at l_ _ _ _ seven fruits and vegetables a day.

c. They are fo_ _ of fish and eat li_ _ _ meals.

d. Okinawan elders enjoy life and don't r_ _ _.

e. Most have very close ti_ _ to family and friends.

5. Listen to the story track 16

Now listen to the story two or three times. Look at the pictures below as you listen.

6. Retell the story

Cover the story and look at the pictures above. Retell the story using the New Words.

7. Answer the questions

About the story...

a. Where is Okinawa?

b. What are the eating habits of the Okinawan elders?

c. Are these eating habits different from yours? How?

d. What do you know about fast food and health?

About you...

e. Would you like to live in Okinawa? Why or why not?

f. What do you do to keep your heart and bones healthy?

g. What foods are you fond of?

h. What changes, if any, do you think you should make to your diet?

8. Learn word partnerships

Study the partnerships below. Complete the sentences so they are true for you.

BE FOND OF		
be fond of	something or someone	**The Okinawans are fond of fish.**
		I'm fond of my neighbors.
	doing something	*I'm fond of reading.*
be really not at all fond of		*My aunt is really fond of me.* *I'm not at all fond of dancing.*

a. I'm fond _____ in the summer.

b. I'm _____ fond of my neighbors.

c. Two foods I'm _____ fond _____ are _____ and _____.

9. Learn word groups

Complete the sentences so they are true. Use words from the picture.

INSIDE THE BODY

lungs
brain
heart
muscles
bones
stomach

a. The _____ sends and receives messages.

b. Exercise makes our _____ bigger.

c. We breathe with our _____.

d. Most people have 206 _____ in their bodies.

10. Take a dictation track 17

Use your own paper to write the dictation. Check your answers on page 86.

11. Complete the story

Use the words from the box to complete the story.

brain	habits	as a result	are fond of	bones	imagine

Young at Heart

CALIFORNIA, USA, and ENGLAND   Can you **(1)** _____ yourself at 104 years old? Will you have fun and continue to learn new things? Meet three unusual elders who are young at heart and, **(2)** _____, are really enjoying their later years.

Daisy Barton, a 104-year-old British woman from Brighton, bought a scooter* for her last birthday. Although she fell off and broke some **(3)** _____ recently, she can't wait to get back on it. "You're never too old for a new adventure," says the great-grandmother.

Eleanor Braver just turned 90. She's the oldest teacher in Los Angeles. "You can live long like me," she tells her teenage students, "if you have healthy **(4)** _____." Her students **(5)** _____ her and say their teacher doesn't seem old at all.

Then there is Gustava Bennett-Burrus, 97, who is going back to school to study computers. "I have always wanted to do this," she says. Bennett-Burrus, who lives in Northern California, stopped going to school when she was eight because she had to help her parents pick cotton in the fields. "I want to use my **(6)** _____," she says. "I always have good ideas."

*scooter: a small motorcycle

 Talk about the stories

Imagine that you and a partner are an Okinawan elder and Daisy Barton. You are meeting for the first time. Tell each other about your lives.

9

Harry Potter Saved Her

1. Read the story

Look at the pictures on these pages. What is the story about? Now read it.

LONDON, ENGLAND **¹**Everyone loves Harry Potter! He is one of the most famous **characters** in the world. His **creator**, J.K. Rowling, is now a successful writer, but life was not always easy for her. **²**Born in 1965, Rowling grew up in a small town in England. She played in the **surrounding** fields, imagining that they were full of **magic**.

³Misfortune hit when Rowling was 15. Her mother became ill and died several years later. **⁴**Rowling had a baby and then her **marriage broke up**. She became deeply **depressed**.

⁵Harry Potter saved her. While sitting on a train in 1990, Rowling got the idea for Harry. "**All at once**, the idea for Harry just appeared in my head … I have never been so excited."

⁶Unemployed and poor, Rowling started writing. She worked extremely hard, writing day after day in a **cafe**, with her baby next to her. **⁷**In 1996, when she tried to sell her first Harry Potter story, 12 publishers* refused it. **⁸**Then she finally **received** good news—the thirteenth publisher had accepted it! "I felt so happy," Rowling said, "that it was going to be a real book on the **shelf** of a bookstore."

———

*publishers: companies that make books

NEW WORDS

character *n*	magic *n*	break up *v*	cafe *n*
creator *n*	misfortune *n*	depressed *adj*	receive *v*
surrounding *adj*	marriage *n*	all at once *adv*	shelf *n*

>> See Glossary on page 92. >>

2. Rate the story

How much did you like it? Mark an ✗.

Not at All   A Lot

① ② ③ ④ ⑤

3. Check your comprehension

Put the sentences in the correct order. Number them 1–7.

a. ___ Rowling wrote every day in a cafe.

b. ___ Harry Potter appeared in her head.

c. ___ Rowling's mother became ill and died.

d. ___ Rowling grew up in England.

e. ___ She became depressed.

f. ___ A publisher finally accepted her book.

g. ___ Her marriage broke up.

4. Check your vocabulary

Complete the sentences with the New Words.

a. Rowling grew up in a small town and played in the surr_ _ _ _ _ _ _ fields, which seemed full of ma_ _ _.

b. Mis_ _ _ _ _ _ _ hit when Rowling's mother became ill.

c. Rowling felt very happy when she re_ _ _ _ _ _ good news from the thirteenth publisher.

d. Now you can find Harry Potter on the sh_ _ _ of almost every bookstore in the world. He is a popular cha_ _ _ _ _ _!

5. Listen to the story 🔘 track 18

Now listen to the story two or three times. Look at the pictures below as you listen.

6. Retell the story

Cover the story and look at the pictures above. Retell the story using the New Words.

7. Answer the questions

About the story...

a. What did Rowling do as a child?

b. When did she first imagine Harry?

c. What difficulties has she had in her life?

d. What does the title of this unit mean?

About you...

e. What question would you like to ask Rowling?

f. Do you like the Harry Potter books or movies? Why or why not?

g. Who is your favorite character in a book or movie?

h. Do you like to write stories? Why or why not?

8. Learn word partnerships

Study the partnerships below. Complete the sentences so they are true for you.

RECEIVE		
receive	good news	***Rowling finally received good news.***
	bad news	*I don't like to receive bad news.*
	an e-mail	*Did you receive an e-mail from me?*
	a gift (from someone)	*I received a great gift from my son.*
	a call	*You'll receive a call from Ann.*
	a grade	*I received a good grade from my teacher.*

a. Yesterday I received _____.

b. I never receive _____ from _____.

c. If I'm lucky, I'll receive _____ from _____.

9. Learn word groups

Complete the sentences so they are true. Use words from the pictures.

READING

a. Every novel has a/an _____.

b. The last novel I read had an interesting _____.

c. You can find a/an _____ and a/an _____ in libraries.

d. The _____ J.K. Rowling wrote a world-famous _____.

10. Take a dictation track 19

Use your own paper to write the dictation. Check your answers on page 86.

11. Complete the story

Use the words from the box to complete the story.

all at once	magic	creator	characters
	depressed	received bad news	

A Well-Loved Character

HOLLYWOOD, USA   One of the most famous **(1)** _____ in the
world is Mickey Mouse. His **(2)** _____,
Walt Disney, began to draw* as a young child. In
1923, when he was 22 years old, Disney arrived
in Hollywood with only $40.00 in his pocket. He
started his own business making cartoons**,
but it was not an easy life.

   In 1928, Walt Disney was riding on a train
from New York to Hollywood. He was
(3) _____. He had **(4)** _____
in New York. His business was in trouble. But as
he was sitting on the train, a mouse appeared in
his head **(5)** _____. It was
(6) _____. Disney spent the rest of the
trip dreaming about the little mouse with big
black ears and red pants. He named his little
mouse "Mortimer," but Disney's wife told him to
use the name "Mickey" instead. A star was born!

   Mickey Mouse was in many popular cartoons in the 1930s and 1940s.
Now he welcomes millions of people every year at Disney parks in Tokyo,
Paris, Florida, and California.

_____

   *draw: to make a picture with a pencil, pen, etc.
   **cartoons: films that are made with drawings

 Talk about the stories

How are the lives of J.K. Rowling and Walt Disney similar? How are they different?

10

Friends on the Wall

1. Read the story

Look at the pictures on these pages.
What is the story about? Now read it.

BERLIN, GERMANY [1]Do you ever feel lonely? Many people do, **especially** those who live by themselves. Holidays can be **particularly** hard for single people without families or companions. [2]Two German women have **developed** something to help solve this problem. It's wallpaper*!

[3]Their special wallpaper shows **life-size** photographs of people doing **routine**, everyday things like eating dinner or sitting on a **sofa**. [4]When you **hang** a "wallpaper friend" in your house or **apartment**, you are no longer alone. "The wallpaper makes you feel like there are other people in the room," says one of the creators, Susanne Schmidt. [5]Schmidt says that a great **advantage** of wallpaper friends is that they always **behave** well. They won't **annoy** you by leaving dirty dishes in the kitchen.

[6]Single people in Germany are crazy about the new wallpaper and are buying lots of it. [7]It is easy to put on or pull off your walls, so you can change "friends" **frequently**. [8]Schmidt is now working on a new kind of wallpaper. It is for couples who are often **apart** and want a life-size **copy** of their husband or wife on the wall. A paper companion is better than none at all!

---

*wallpaper: special paper that you use to cover the walls of a room

NEW WORDS

especially adv	**life-size** adj	**hang** v	**behave** v	**apart** adv
particularly adv	**routine** adj	**apartment** n	**annoy** v	**copy** n
develop v	**sofa** n	**advantage** n	**frequently** adv	

>> See Glossary on page 92. >>

2. Rate the story

How much did you like it? Mark an ✗.

Not at All   A Lot

① ② ③ ④ ⑤

3. Check your comprehension

Check (✓) the endings that are true.

a. The new wallpaper

___ is for lonely people.

___ was developed in Spain.

___ has small pictures on it.

___ shows people doing routine things.

___ is popular in Germany.

b. "Wallpaper friends"

___ are life-size.

___ are real people.

___ can be hung on a wall.

___ behave well.

___ can be changed frequently.

4. Check your vocabulary

Complete the sentences with the New Words.

a. Many people feel lonely, esp_ _ _ _ _ _ _ those who live alone.

b. The German wallpaper shows life-_ _ _ _ photos of people doing rou_ _ _ _ things.

c. When you h_ _ _ a "wallpaper friend" in your ap_ _ _ _ _ _ _, you are no longer alone.

d. The newest wallpaper is for couples who are often ap_ _ _ and want a c_ _ _ of their husband or wife on the wall.

5. Listen to the story track 20

Now listen to the story two or three times. Look at the pictures below as you listen.

6. Retell the story

Cover the story and look at the pictures above. Retell the story using the New Words.

7. Answer the questions

About the story…

a. What can be particularly hard for single people?

b. What are the advantages of "wallpaper friends"? Who developed them?

c. What kind of pictures are on the wallpaper?

About you…

d. What do you hang on your walls?

e. Would you like "wallpaper friends" in your home? Why or why not?

f. What helps you when you feel lonely?

g. Do your friends ever annoy you? How?

8. Learn word partnerships

Study the partnerships below. Complete the sentences so they are true for you.

ANNOY	
annoy someone by doing something	***Wallpaper friends won't annoy you by leaving dirty dishes.*** *John annoys me by talking too much.* *I annoy my friends by calling late at night.*
something annoys someone	*Loud music annoys her.* *Traffic jams annoy me.* *Rude people annoy my father.*

a. _____ annoys me.

b. Sometimes I annoy my family by _____.

c. Some of my friends annoy me by _____.

9. Learn word groups

Complete the sentences so they are true for you. Use words from the picture.

A LIVING ROOM

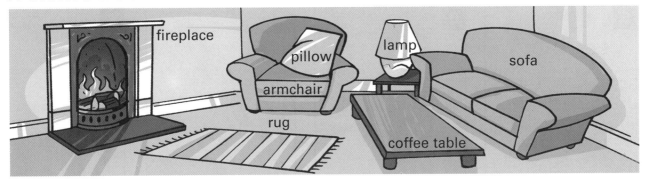

a. In my living room, there's a/an _____ and a/an _____.

b. There's no _____ in my living room.

c. I'd like to have a/an _____ in my living room.

10. Take a dictation track 21

Use your own paper to write the dictation. Check your answers on page 86.

11. Complete the story

Use the words from the box to complete the story.

behave	developed	armchair	apartment
advantage	particularly	frequently	

No Longer Lonely

CHICAGO, USA "I'm home! Where's my Angel?" Barbara calls when she walks into her **(1)** _____. Her cat runs from behind the sofa or **(2)** _____ to welcome her. "Angel makes me happy," Barbara says. "She's a good companion."

Barbara lives alone. When her husband died several years ago, Barbara was **(3)** _____ lonely. The house felt empty. "The loneliness* goes away when I'm holding Angel," says Barbara. "I've **(4)** _____ so much love for her."

Scientists** say that the biggest health problem for older people is not cancer or heart disease, but loneliness. Now scientists are showing that dogs and cats can help. Older people who live alone are happier living with an animal. Another big **(5)** _____ is that they stay healthier and live longer.

"Angel doesn't always **(6)** _____ well," says Barbara. "But she needs me, and that's **(7)** _____ important to me now."
_____

* loneliness: being lonely (with no other people)
** scientists: people who study science (the study of natural things)

Talk about the stories

Which would you prefer—to have a "wallpaper friend" or an animal? Why?

11

Ads on Heads

1. Read the story

Look at the pictures on these pages.
What is the story about? Now read it.

LONDON, ENGLAND **¹Advertisements**, or ads, are everywhere, telling us to buy, buy, buy. They're on TV and the Internet. Ads are on buses, trains, and **ugly** billboards*. You can't get away from them.

²But now advertising has reached a new **level**—ads are appearing on **human** heads! **³**An ad agency** in London is **hiring** college students as human billboards and putting washable ads on their **foreheads**. **⁴**The agency pays about $7.00 an hour, and many students think it's a simple, fun way to earn money.

⁵The agency is careful about who it hires. The young people who wear the ads have to be fashionable and **attractive**. **⁶**They also have to stay in crowded areas during the hours they "work." They can go to **local** cafes or **clubs** during working hours, but they can't sit in a library.

⁷Stuart Charles, 28, wore an ad on his forehead for a week. Everyone had an **opinion** about it. "Some friends were laughing," he says. "Then they realized I was getting **cash** and they weren't." **⁸Later on** Charles went to a movie, where people were unfriendly. "They were probably thinking that capitalism*** has gone too far," Charles explains.

---

  *billboards: very large pictures outside that show
    an advertisement
 **ad agency: a company that makes advertisements
***capitalism: an economic system based on
    private business

NEW WORDS

advertisement *n*	level *n*	hire *v*	attractive *adj*	club *n*	cash *n*
ugly *adj*	human *adj*	forehead *n*	local *adj*	opinion *n*	later on *adv*

>> See Glossary on page 93. >>

2. Rate the story

How much did you like it? Mark an ✗.

Not at All   A Lot
① ② ③ ④ ⑤

3. Check your comprehension

Check (✓) the endings that are true.

a. Ads are on

___ trains and buses.

___ ugly billboards.

___ people's heads.

b. A London ad agency

___ puts washable ads on foreheads.

___ pays about $7.00 an hour to human billboards.

___ hires anyone as a human billboard.

c. Students wearing the ads

___ are fashionable and attractive.

___ earn money while reading at the library.

___ earn cash while sitting in cafes or clubs.

4. Check your vocabulary

Complete the sentences with the New Words.

a. Advertising has reached a new le_ _ _. You can now find ads on human _ _ _ _heads!

b. A London ad agency is hiring att_ _ _ _ _ _ _ young people to wear the ads.

c. The young people can go to l_ _ _ _ cafes or _ _ _bs during working hours.

d. When Stuart Charles wore an ad on his head, everyone who saw it had an op_ _ _ _ _ _ about it.

5. Listen to the story 🔘 track 22

Now listen to the story two or three times. Look at the pictures below as you listen.

6. Retell the story

Cover the story and look at the pictures above. Retell the story using the New Words.

7. Answer the questions

About the story…

a. Why has advertising reached a new level?

b. Why do students want the ads on their foreheads?

c. What kind of students does the agency hire?

d. Would you like to wear an ad on your forehead for $7.00 an hour? Why or why not?

About you…

e. Are you a human billboard? How often do you wear clothes with ads on them?

f. Have you bought something recently because of an ad? What?

g. Name an ad that you have seen recently. Do you think it is honest?

h. Do you think capitalism has gone too far? Why or why not?

8. Learn word partnerships

Study the partnerships below. Complete the sentences so they are true for you.

OPINION	
have an **opinion** about something	***Everyone had an opinion about the ad.*** *I have a strong opinion about that movie.*
agree disagree | with someone's **opinion**	*I agree with your opinion.* *He often disagrees with Bob's opinion.*
In my **opinion**,…	*In my opinion, you should work harder.*

a. I often agree _____'s opinion.

b. I have a strong opinion about _____.

c. In my _____, people should _____.

9. Learn word groups

Complete the sentences so they are true for you. Use words from the pictures.

WAYS OF PAYING

a bill   a coin   cash   a check   a credit card

a. I usually pay for books and magazines with _____.

b. Right now I have _____(s) in my wallet or purse.

c. The last time I went to a restaurant, I paid for the meal with _____.

10. Take a dictation track 23

Use your own paper to write the dictation. Check your answers on page 87.

11. Complete the story

Use the words from the box to complete the story.

hiring	cash	in my opinion	advertisement	human	ugly

MAN WEAR$ AD$ ON HEAD FOR CA$H

KANSAS CITY, MO., USA James Nelson wanted to start his own business, but he didn't have enough **(1)** _____. So he became a **(2)** _____ billboard.

In 2003, Nelson entered a competition on the Internet and won $7,000. In order to get the money, Nelson has to wear an **(3)** _____ on his head—for five long years! The Texas Internet company

that is **(4)** _____ Nelson has written its Internet address in large letters across the back of Nelson's head and neck.

Nelson had to cut off most of his hair. Then someone wrote the ad with permanent ink* on Nelson's head. It took more than four hours. Nelson says that nobody has done this before. "And it's better than going to the bank for a business loan**," he adds proudly. "**(5)** _____, it's not so **(6)** _____," said an Internet user about Nelson's head.

_____

*permanent ink: a colored liquid that does not wash off
**loan: money that someone lends you

 Talk about the stories

How are Stuart Charles and James Nelson similar? How are they different?

12

Fashion Star

1. Read the story

Look at the pictures on these pages.
What is the story about? Now read it.

PARIS, FRANCE **¹**Not so long ago, Ji Haye was a **confused** Korean teenager, **uncertain** about her future. She jumped from one subject* to the next at universities in Seoul and Japan. **²**Then she went to fashion school. "This is it!" she thought and traveled to Paris, **eager** to make her **fortune**.

³Life there wasn't easy. For eight years she worked under famous **designers**, sewing their clothes, not hers. Many young designers just **give up**, but not Ji Haye. **⁴**She went home at night, **drew** her own **designs**, and went on dreaming.

⁵Then one day she received an invitation to show her clothes at a haute couture fashion show** in Paris, along with big names like Chanel and Dior. **⁶**Designers **prepare** a whole year for this 15-minute show, and most have help from the best workers. **⁷**"But … there was no one to help me," says Ji Haye. She did every **detail** herself. She worked 20-hour days, pushing and pulling a **needle** until her arms were swollen***.

⁸Now Ji Haye is a star in Paris, famous for her colorful clothes using Korean **material** and **traditional** Korean designs. She says it's hard work to stay on top. "I always live like I'm standing at the edge of a cliff."

---

* subject: something you study in school, like math or history

** haute couture fashion show: a special event where people look at new clothes

*** swollen: fatter or thicker than usual

NEW WORDS

confused *adj*	**fortune** *n*	**draw** *v*	**detail** *n*	**traditional** *adj*
uncertain *adj*	**designer** *n*	**design** *n*	**needle** *n*	
eager *adj*	**give up** *v*	**prepare** *v*	**material** *n*	

>> See Glossary on page 93. >>

2. Rate the story

How much did you like it? Mark an ✗.

Not at All   A Lot
①   ②   ③   ④   ⑤

3. Check your comprehension

Put the sentences in the correct order. Number them 1–6.

a. ____ She went to fashion school.

b. ____ She became a fashion star.

c. ____ She traveled to Paris to make her fortune.

d. ____ Ji Haye went to universities in Seoul and Japan.

e. ____ For a year, she worked 20-hour days for a haute couture fashion show.

f. ____ She sewed clothes for famous designers for eight years.

4. Check your vocabulary

Complete the sentences with the New Words.

a. As a teenager, Ji Haye was unce_ _ _ _ _ and conf_ _ _ _ about her future.

b. In Paris, she d_ _ _ her own designs at night and didn't g_ _ _ up.

c. She _ _ _pared a whole year for her first fashion show, doing every det_ _ _ herself.

d. She uses trad_ _ _ _ _ _ _ Korean designs and _ _ _ _rials in her clothes.

5. Listen to the story track 24

Now listen to the story two or three times. Look at the pictures below as you listen.

6. Retell the story

Cover the story and look at the pictures above. Retell the story using the New Words.

7. Answer the questions

About the story...

a. Why did Ji Haye travel to Paris?

b. What did she do there during her first eight years?

c. How did she prepare for her first fashion show?

d. Do you think Ji Haye has an interesting job? Why or why not?

About you...

e. Do you like fashion? What kind?

f. Do you think clothes tell something about people? If so, what?

g. What kind of work do you want to do in the future?

h. How many hours a day are you willing to work to be successful?

8. Learn word partnerships

Study the partnerships below. Complete the sentences so they are true for you.

GIVE UP		
give up		***Many designers lose hope, but Ji Haye didn't give up.*** *Learning French is hard, but I won't give up.*
give up	(something)	*I should give up junk food.* *I gave up television for a week.*
	(doing something)	*He's going to give up drinking soda.* *I gave up eating sweets last week.*

a. _____ is difficult, but I will not give up.

b. I should give up _____.

c. I gave up eating _____ because _____.

9. Learn word groups

Complete the sentences so they are true for you. Use words from the picture.

SEWING

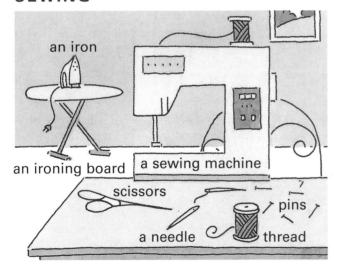

an iron

an ironing board | a sewing machine

scissors

pins

a needle   thread

a. I often use _____.

b. I never use _____.

c. To sew on a button, I use _____.

10. Take a dictation 🔘 track 25

Use your own paper to write the dictation. Check your answers on page 87.

11. Complete the story

Use the words from the box to complete the story.

| designs | prepared | details | give up | eager | materials | traditional |

Men in Skirts? Why Not?

NEW YORK CITY, USA

On a cold winter morning in 2004, a hundred men marched to the Metropolitan Museum* of Art in New York. They were all wearing skirts. The museum had **(1)** _____ a fashion exhibit** called "Bravehearts: Men in Skirts," and the marchers were **(2)** _____ to show their support*** for the idea of men in skirts.

One of the marchers was David Johnson, a history teacher from New York. "We're men," he said. "Men who want the freedom to wear a skirt." The marchers agreed that modern fashion **(3)** _____ for men's clothes are boring. "If women can wear pants, why can't we wear skirts?" they asked.

The museum exhibit showed the history of men's clothes. In the past, men around the world wore many kinds of **(4)** _____ clothes–kimonos, grass skirts, long dresses, and short Scottish skirts. Men's clothes were often made from beautiful **(5)** _____ and had many rich **(6)** _____. "Why should we **(7)** _____ wearing beautiful clothes just because we're men?" one of the marchers asked.

---

* museum: a building where people can look at old, unusual, or interesting things
** exhibit: a special group of things in a museum
*** support: help for someone or something

 Talk about the stories

What new things did you learn about fashion in this unit? Would you like to be a fashion designer? Why or why not?

1. Match the words with the pictures.

___ **a.** professor   ___ **d.** club

___ **b.** needle   ___ **e.** apartment

___ **c.** material   ___ **f.** forehead

1.

2.

3.

4.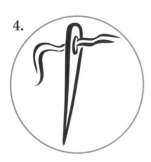

5.

6.

2. Write the words in the picture.

| cash | advertisement | sofa | shelf | cafe | bone |

3. Are the sentences true or false? Check (✓) the correct box.

		T	F
a.	Eating fruit is a good habit.	☐	☐
b.	The creator of the Mickey Mouse character is Walt Disney.	☐	☐
c.	It snows frequently in Hawaii.	☐	☐
d.	Your forehead is below your eyes.	☐	☐
e.	Heart attacks are rare in Okinawa.	☐	☐
f.	Human bodies have at least 500 bones.	☐	☐

4. Cross out the item that *cannot* complete each sentence.

a. Eva and her friends plan to meet at _____.

    1. her apartment   2. their local cafe   3. the copy   4. the club

b. Robert does not want to give up his _____.

    1. bad habits   2. freedom   3. misfortune   4. favorite hobby

c. Tom did not pass his exams. He feels _____ about the future.

    1. ugly   2. confused   3. depressed   4. uncertain

d. Sara is not in good health and does not go to school _____.

    1. at present   2. frequently   3. as a result   4. especially

e. Bruce is an excellent _____.

    1. designer   2. magic   3. professor   4. boss

5. Match the definitions with the words.

a. design ____		1.	success; good luck; a lot of money
b. develop ____		2.	being all around something
c. fortune ____		3.	to speak a little about something
d. level ____		4.	to work on something and make it more complete
e. advantage ____		5.	a drawing that shows how to make something
f. mention ____		6.	doing something as a job for money
g. professional ____		7.	something that helps you or is useful
h. surrounding ____		8.	a particular standard or quantity

6. Use the words from the box to complete the sentences.

| give up | routine | human | tester | regular | broke up |
| at present | though | life-size | hiring | depressed | ties |

a. Andy Alamano, a video game _____, earns $40,000 a year _____.

b. The Okinawans stay healthy because they are _____ eaters of tofu, fruits, and vegetables and have close _____ to their families.

c. After J.K. Rowling's marriage _____, she became _____.

d. The special wallpaper from two German designers shows _____ photos of people doing _____, everyday things.

e. An ad agency in London is _____ college students as _____ billboards.

f. Ji Haye did not _____. Many fashion designers did, _____.

7. Use the words from the box to complete the story.

| all at once | received | according to |
| particularly | at least | cash | later on |

Thief Sends Red Roses

GUANGZHOU, CHINA

(1) _____ the *China Daily*, a thief sent roses to a young woman after stealing her purse. The woman, Ma, was walking down the street.
(2) _____, a man on a bicycle rode by and pulled her bag off her arm. Ma lost
(3) _____, some photos, and her passport.
(4) _____, when she remembered that her phone was in her bag, Ma sent it a message. She asked the thief to return
(5) _____ the passport

and photos. Ma soon got her passport and photos back. She also (6) _____ a gift of 11 red roses from the criminal. He was a (7) _____ kind thief!

8. Check (✓) *yes* or *no*.

	Yes	No
a. I am always rushing.	☐	☐
b. Someone in my family has had a heart attack.	☐	☐
c. I usually pay attention to details.	☐	☐
d. I like the idea of marriage.	☐	☐
e. I like to hang pictures on my walls.	☐	☐

	Yes	No
f. I always behave well at school.	☐	☐
g. I learn at least five new English words a day.	☐	☐
h. I like to prepare traditional foods from my country.	☐	☐
i. I usually eat light meals.	☐	☐
j. I like to draw.	☐	☐

9. Complete the sentences so they are true for you.

a. My favorite hobby is _____.

b. The most attractive thing about me is _____.

c. I hope I have the opportunity to _____.

d. _____ annoys me.

e. I am very fond of _____.

f. In my opinion, children should _____.

g. I would like to earn _____ a year.

h. I often imagine that I will _____ in the future.

10. Fill in the chart with names of classmates. Try to write a different name in each blank. Walk around the room and ask questions such as:

Would you like to earn a fortune?
Do you like to draw pictures of people?

The winner is the first person to fill in seven blanks.

FIND SOMEONE WHO...

a. would like to earn a fortune.

b. likes to draw pictures of people.

c. thinks that pizza is more delicious than anything else.

d. has some cash in his or her pocket.

e. is eager to learn English.

f. is always rushing in the morning.

g. often goes to a local club.

h. likes to lie on the sofa while watching TV.

i. was apart from his or her family last summer.

j. often receives letters from friends.

13

Cat and Couple Are Homeless

1. Read the story

Look at the pictures on these pages.
What is the story about? Now read it.

GERMANY ¹Robbie was always a good **pet**—sweet and playful. But the lovable little cat recently destroyed the home of a German couple. How did this **disaster** happen?

²One evening, Robbie was playing in the upstairs bathtub*. **By accident**, he turned on the **faucet**. ³Elsie and Walter Kochentopf were cooking dinner in the kitchen when they noticed something strange. Water was coming down through the **ceiling**. ⁴Then they saw a river of water running down the stairs all the way into the **basement**. ⁵The couple ran downstairs to try to save their things—boxes of books, papers, and clothes. There was water everywhere, so they began to empty the basement. ⁶**Meanwhile**, their dinner was still cooking on the **stove** in the kitchen. They had completely forgotten about it! ⁷It started to burn, and the **flames** jumped quickly around the kitchen. The whole room and a nearby hallway were completely destroyed.

⁸Fortunately, no one was **injured**. The Kochentopfs are now homeless, waiting until they can **repair** all the fire and water damage. And Robbie? He has been **forgiven** and cannot wait to get back home.

---

*bathtub: the thing you take a bath in

NEW WORDS

pet *n*	**by accident** *adv*	**ceiling** *n*	**meanwhile** *adv*	**flame** *n*	**repair** *v*
disaster *n*	**faucet** *n*	**basement** *n*	**stove** *n*	**injure** *v*	**forgive** *v*

>> See Glossary on page 94. >>

2. Rate the story

How much did you like it? Mark an ✗.

Not at All   A Lot
① ② ③ ④ ⑤

3. Check your comprehension

Put the sentences in the correct order. Number them 1–7.

a. ___ Flames jumped quickly around the kitchen.

b. ___ Their cat turned on a bathtub faucet upstairs.

c. ___ Their dinner began to burn.

d. ___ Water started running down the stairs and into the basement.

e. ___ The Kochentopfs were cooking dinner in the kitchen.

f. ___ The couple ran down to save their boxes of books and clothes.

g. ___ The whole kitchen was destroyed.

4. Check your vocabulary

Complete the sentences with the New Words.

a. The Kochentopfs' p_ _ destroyed their home by acc_ _ _ _ _.

b. Water from the upstairs fa_ _ _ _ ran all the way down to the _ _ _ ment.

c. Fl_ _ _ _ from the st_ _ _ burned down the kitchen.

d. The Kochentopfs have _ _ _given the cat and will re_ _ _ _ the house.

5. Listen to the story track 26

Now listen to the story two or three times. Look at the pictures below as you listen.

6. Retell the story

Cover the story and look at the pictures above. Retell the story using the New Words.

7. Answer the questions

About the story...

a. How did the disaster begin?

b. When did the couple realize that something strange was happening?

c. Why did the couple forget that dinner was on the stove?

d. Does this story have a happy or a sad ending? Why?

About you...

e. Do you have a pet or want a pet? What kind?

f. What have you damaged or destroyed by accident?

g. Has there ever been a disaster in your home? What happened?

h. What can you do to stay safe in your home?

8. Learn word partnerships

Study the partnerships below. Complete the sentences so they are true for you.

REPAIR		
repair	the damage	**The Kochentopfs will repair the damage.**
	a broken bike	*I have to repair my broken bike.*
	an old computer	*She's not going to repair her old computer.*
	damaged walls	*We repaired our damaged walls.*
	shoes	*Can you repair these shoes?*

a. I have to repair _____.

b. I'm not going to repair my broken _____.

c. My family recently repaired our damaged _____.

9. Learn word groups

Complete the sentences so they are true for you. Use words from the picture.

A KITCHEN

a. In my kitchen, the stove is next to the _____.

b. I'd like a new _____ in my kitchen.

c. I use the _____ every day, but not the _____.

10. Take a dictation track 27

Use your own paper to write the dictation. Check your answers on page 87.

11. Complete the story

Use the words from the box to complete the story.

disaster	meanwhile	ceiling	flames
repair the damage		injured	water heater

WHAT ARE THE CHANCES?

GREAT YARMOUTH, ENGLAND   Daphne Jones needs a new bathroom. Her old one exploded. The walls and the **(1)** _____ were destroyed. How did this **(2)** _____ happen? It's a strange story.

One morning, Jones put dirty clothes into the washing machine in her bathroom and turned it on. Then she left for work. There were scissors and a can of spray paint* sitting on the machine. When the machine began to shake a little, it threw the can of paint on the floor. The machine shook a

little more and the scissors flew off. They landed right in the can of paint. Fumes** started coming out of the can.

(3) _____, a nearby water heater turned on. The **(4)** _____ from the water heater mixed*** with the fumes from the paint can. The **(5)** _____ exploded violently, destroying the whole bathroom and really scaring the neighbors.

Fortunately, no one was **(6)** _____ in the accident. Jones plans to **(7)** _____. "The chances that this could happen are one in a million," said the fire chief.

---

* spray paint: a liquid in a can that you can use to change the color of
  your walls or your furniture
** fumes: smoke or air that smells bad
*** mixed: joined with

Talk about the stories

Imagine that you and a partner are Elsie Kochentopf and Daphne Jones. You are meeting for the first time. Tell each other about the disasters in your homes.

Ice Man

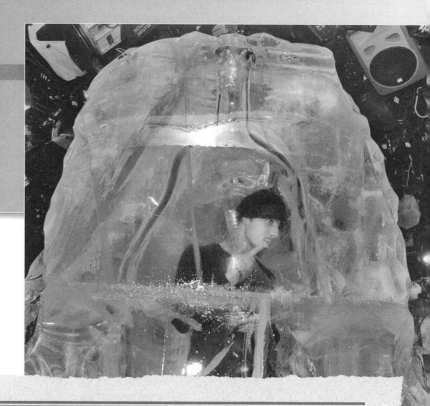

1. Read the story

Look at the pictures on these pages.
What is the story about? Now read it.

NEW YORK CITY, USA [1]Imagine standing inside a thick **block** of ice for three days. That's what performance artist* David Blaine did in 2000. "I felt like I had lost my **mind**," he said later.

[2]Blaine was **trapped** in ice in the middle of Times Square, wearing only boots, pants, a shirt, and a hat. Only two inches **separated** his body from the ice. [3]He had to stay awake because if his **chest** fell against the ice, he could **freeze** to death. [4]Air and water came through tubes**. For Blaine this was a test to see how much his body and mind could take. [5]New Yorkers and tourists **encouraged** him to go on by holding up **signs**. [6]After 62 hours, Blaine couldn't take it any longer. He screamed to get out. "I thought that I had died," he said later. His companions **broke open** the ice and Blaine stepped out. It was finally **over**! Blaine **recovered** in the hospital.

[7]Blaine has done many other unusual stunts. In 1999, he was buried alive for seven days, and in 2003, he hung over London in a glass box for 44 days without food. [8]Blaine has many fans***. "It would be a **dull** world," said one, "if people didn't **occasionally** do something **silly**."

---

* performance artist: a person who shows his or her talent to others in an unusual way
** tubes: long, thin plastic pipes
*** fans: people who really like somebody famous

block *n*	separate *v*	encourage *v*	over *adv*	occasionally *adv*
mind *n*	chest *n*	sign *n*	recover *v*	silly *adj*
trap *v*	freeze *v*	break open *v*	dull *adj*	

>> See Glossary on page 94. >>

2. Rate the story

How much did you like it? Mark an ✗.

Not at All   A Lot
1   2   3   4   5

3. Check your comprehension

Correct five mistakes in the story summary.

In 2000, David Blaine stood inside a block of stone for three days in the middle of London. Food and water came through tubes. People encouraged him by holding up signs. When Blaine screamed to get out of the ice, his companions broke it open and Blaine fell out. He recovered at home. "I thought that I had died," he said later.

4. Check your vocabulary

Complete the sentences with the New Words.

a. Blaine was _ _ _ _ped in a thick b_ _ _ _ of ice.

b. If his ch_ _ _ fell against the ice, he could fr_ _ _ _ to death.

c. When it was all o_ _ _, Blaine went to the hospital to re_ _ _ _ _.

d. "It would be a d_ _ _ world," says a fan, "if people didn't occasionally do something s_ _ _ _."

5. Listen to the story   track 28

Now listen to the story two or three times. Look at the pictures below as you listen.

6. Retell the story

Cover the story and look at the pictures above. Retell the story using the New Words.

7. Answer the questions

About the story…

a. Where did Blaine spend three days?

b. Why did he have to stay awake?

c. Who encouraged him? How?

d. What happened after Blaine screamed to get out?

About you…

e. How long do you think you could stand in a block of ice?

f. Which of Blaine's three stunts seems the scariest to you?

g. Have you ever done anything really strange or silly?

h. Who encourages you to try new things in life?

8. Learn word partnerships

Study the partnerships below. Complete the sentences so they are true for you.

ENCOURAGE		
encourage someone to do something		**Blaine's fans encouraged him to go on.** *My mother encourages me to play the piano.* *He encouraged Alice to sing.*
strongly gently	encourage	*My boss strongly encouraged me to arrive on time.* *Our teacher gently encourages us to speak English.*

a. My English teacher encourages me to _____.

b. When I was a child, _____ encouraged me _____.

c. My parents strongly _____ to _____.

9. Learn word groups

Complete the sentences so they are true. Use words from the picture.

THE BODY

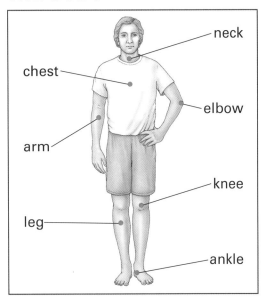

neck
chest
elbow
arm
knee
leg
ankle

a. The _____ is between the head and shoulders.

b. The _____ is in the middle of the arm.

c. The ankle and _____ are on the _____.

d. I have two _____ _____s.

10. Take a dictation 🔘 track 29

Use your own paper to write the dictation. Check your answers on page 87.

11. Complete the story

Use the words from the box to complete the story.

mind	over	blocks	encouraged her to
recover	arms	freeze	occasionally

Swimming in Ice

ANTARCTICA Lynne Cox has done something that is hard to believe. In 2002, she swam for 25 minutes in the Antarctic Ocean–the coldest water on earth. Cox has taught herself to push pain out of her **(1)** _____.

Wearing just a bathing suit*, she jumped from a boat and began swimming in the icy water. The water was $0°$ C. (If you put your finger in this water, it burns!) With her strong

(2) _____ and legs, Cox swam through

(3) _____ of ice. Penguins** swam beside and under her. She **(4)** _____ got confused, but her friends in a nearby boat

(5) _____ continue.

After swimming 1.6 kilometers, Cox reached the shores of Antarctica. Her swim was

(6) _____! Friends put blankets around her and lay on top of her to make her warm. Cox slowly began to **(7)** _____.

Cox has always liked cold-water swimming. In 1987, she was the first person to swim from Alaska to Russia. Now she is the only person who has swum in the Antarctic Ocean. Doctors are still trying to understand why she does not **(8)** _____ in water that could kill most people. Cox says the swim was painful, but "fantastic."

_____

* bathing suit: something people wear when they go swimming
** penguins: black and white birds that live in very cold places

 Talk about the stories

Imagine that you and a partner are David Blaine and Lynne Cox. You are meeting for the first time. Tell each other about the time you've spent in ice.

15

The Amazing Sun

1. Read the story

Look at the pictures on these pages.
What is the story about? Now read it.

ALBERTA, CANADA [1]Everyone loves a sunny room. But did you know that a bright room can make you healthier, happier, and more hard-working? **Amazing** new **research** is teaching us about the **effects** of natural **light**.

[2]Daylight is important in schools. Canadian research **suggests** that students do better on tests in sunny, bright schools. [3]Students are **absent** less often in these schools, too. [4]Even more surprisingly, children seem to grow taller in schools with lots of natural light.

[5]Sunlight is also good for business. The **use** of natural light instead of **electric** light makes customers spend more money in stores. One popular American store put in skylights* and, as a result, business is up 40 percent. [6]In offices, workers who have windows near their desks work harder than those who don't. They also miss fewer days of work.

[7]Sunlight is good for your health. In his book, *Sunlight*, Dr. Zane Kime **advises** readers to get plenty of it. According to Kime, the sun's light gives you more **energy** and **causes** your heart rate** to go down. [8]And with more windows, you use less electricity, which is good for Mother Earth. So open up your **curtains** and let the sun shine in!

---

* skylights: windows in the roof or ceiling
** heart rate: how fast a person's heart beats

NEW WORDS

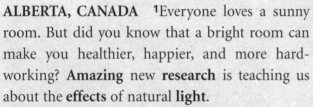

amazing *adj*	**effect** *n*	**suggest** *v*	**use** *n*	**advise** *v*	**cause** *v*
research *n*	**light** *n*	**absent** *adj*	**electric** *adj*	**energy** *n*	**curtain** *n*

>> See Glossary on page 95. >>

2. Rate the story

How much did you like it? Mark an ✗.

Not at All   A Lot

1   2   3   4   5

3. Check your comprehension

Match the first and second parts of the sentences.

a. Research suggests that students ___

b. Workers who have windows ___

c. When an American store put in skylights, business ___

d. Dr. Zane Kime advises readers to ___

e. The sun's light ___

1. work harder than those who don't.

2. went up a lot.

3. get a lot of sunlight to stay healthy.

4. causes your heart rate to go down.

5. are absent less in sunny schools.

4. Check your vocabulary

Complete the sentences with the New Words.

a. Students in sunny schools are a_ _ _ _ _ less often.

b. The u_ _ of natural light rather than ele_ _ _ _ _ light makes people spend more money in stores.

c. Because the sun's light gives you e_ _ _ _ _, Dr. Kime adv_ _ _ _ you to get plenty of it.

d. So open up your cur_ _ _ _ _ and let the sunlight in!

5. Listen to the story track 30

Now listen to the story two or three times. Look at the pictures below as you listen.

6. Retell the story

Cover the story and look at the pictures above. Retell the story using the New Words.

7. Answer the questions

About the story…

a. What are three advantages of sunlight?

b. What are the effects of natural light in schools?

c. What happened when an American store put in skylights?

d. What happens when office workers sit near windows?

About you…

e. How much natural light is there in your school?

f. Do you think there is enough sunlight in your life? Why or why not?

g. How does sunlight make you feel?

h. Think about a business in your neighborhood. Are the workers getting enough light? Why or why not?

8. Learn word partnerships

Study the partnerships below. Complete the sentences so they are true for you.

ADVISE	
advise someone to do something	**Dr. Kime advises readers to get plenty of sunlight.** *My doctor advises me to eat healthy food.* *Her parents advised her to go to college.*
strongly gently advise	*My boss strongly advises me to take the trip.* *Dan's mother gently advised him to get more rest.*

a. When I was young, _____ advised me to _____.

b. My English teacher advises students _____.

c. I _____ my friend to _____.

9. Learn word groups

Complete the sentences so they are true. Use words from the pictures.

LIGHT

   lightbulb   light switch   flashlight   spotlight   streetlight   traffic light

a. I use a _____ to turn on an electric light.

b. You can find a _____ in a lamp.

c. Actors are often in a _____.

d. When people go camping, they often bring a _____.

10. Take a dictation  track 31

Use your own paper to write the dictation. Check your answers on page 87.

11. Complete the story

Use the words from the box to complete the story.

suggests	causes	research	effect	amazing	advise

Amazing Laughter

MARYLAND, USA   How often do you laugh? Did you know that laughter* is like medicine? New research by doctors at the University of Maryland **(1)** _____ that laughter can be good for your heart. People who laugh a lot seem to have less heart disease. Doctors are not sure how this happens, but they are very interested.

Laughter can be useful for sick people, too. **(2)** _____ shows that when people laugh a lot, they feel less pain. Some hospitals invite clowns** to come in to help sick children laugh more.

Healthy five-year-old children laugh about 300 times a day. But most adults laugh only 17 times a day. What **(3)** _____ this **(4)** _____ change? Does our daily life change us into sad people? Do adults think that playing and fun are only for children? Here is what some doctors **(5)** _____: Remember to have fun. Be silly. Watch funny videos. Make friends with people who laugh.

Then see what a good **(6)** _____ laughter has on you!

---

 * laughter: the sound people make when they are happy
 ** clowns: people who wear funny clothes and make people laugh

 Talk about the stories

How are the effects of laughter and sunlight similar? Do you get enough of each? What can you do to get more?

16

Animal Artists

1. Read the story

Look at the pictures on these pages.
What is the story about? Now read it.

QUEBEC, CANADA   ¹Tom loves to **paint** with a brush. His **paintings** explode with **feeling**. ²Binky **would rather** paint with his fingers and feet. He smiles the whole time that he is working. Binky and Tom are **artists**, but they're also chimpanzees*! ³These chimps and four of their friends have shown their work in galleries** in the Canadian cities of Toronto and Montreal. ⁴Many people have enjoyed their work. "It's so strong and **sensitive**," said one person. "You can really see their feelings." Their work sold, too. Buyers paid between $500 and $1,800 for a painting.

⁵Before they became artists, the chimps had a **cruel** life. They were used for many years as test animals in **laboratories** and had become weak and sick. "It's so sad what happened to the chimps," says a Montreal art buyer.

⁶Now the chimps are in a better **situation**, living happily on Gloria Grow's farm with llamas*** and other animals. ⁷The clever chimps can use sign language and **tools**. They also enjoy watching TV and hanging **upside-down** in trees. ⁸Since the chimps get bored so easily, Grow decided to make their lives better by giving them a hobby. "Binky gets this great big smile on his face," she says, "when you come near him with the **paints**."

---

* chimpanzees: animals with no tails; similar to monkeys
** galleries: businesses that show and sell art
*** llamas: South American animals that are like horses and used to carry things

NEW WORDS

paint *v*	would rather *v*	cruel *adj*	tool *n*
painting *n*	artist *n*	laboratory *n*	upside-down *adv*
feeling *n*	sensitive *adj*	situation *n*	paint *n*

>> See Glossary on page 95. >>

2. Rate the story

How much did you like it? Mark an ✗.

Not at All   A Lot
① ② ③ ④ ⑤

3. Check your comprehension

Put the sentences in the correct order. Number them 1–6.

a. ___ Their work was put in a gallery.

b. ___ The chimps lived in laboratories.

c. ___ Grow wanted to make their lives better, so she gave them paints.

d. ___ The chimps became artists.

e. ___ People bought the chimps' paintings.

f. ___ They moved to Gloria Grow's farm.

4. Check your vocabulary

Complete the sentences with the New Words.

a. Tom p_ _ _ _ _ with a brush, but Binky would r_ _ _ _ _ use his fingers.

b. Before the chimps began to make pa_ _ _ _ _ _ s, they had a cr_ _ _ life.

c. Now they are in a better sit_ _ _ _ _ _.

d. The chimps also like to use t_ _ _s and hang upside-_ _ _ _ in trees.

5. Listen to the story   track 32

Now listen to the story two or three times. Look at the pictures below as you listen.

6. Retell the story

Cover the story and look at the pictures above. Retell the story using the New Words.

7. Answer the questions

About the story…

a. Why were the chimps weak and sick?

b. How do Tom and Binky like to paint?

c. How much do people pay for their work?

d. What else do the chimps do on the farm?

About you…

e. Do you think animals should be used in laboratories? Why or why not?

f. Do you think animals have feelings? Why or why not?

g. Are you an artist? What do you do?

h. Who is your favorite painter?

8. Learn word partnerships

Study the partnerships below. Complete the sentences so they are true for you.

WOULD RATHER	
would (much) rather do something	than (do) another thing.
Binky would rather paint with his fingers	**than (paint) with a brush.**
I would rather drink cola	*than (drink) milk.*
I would rather study music	*than (study) math.*
I'd much rather walk to school	*than take the bus.*
I'd much rather cook a meal	*than wash dishes.*

a. I would rather eat _____ than _____.

b. I'd _____ watch _____ than _____.

c. I'd much rather _____.

9. Learn word groups

Complete the sentences so they are true for you. Use words from the pictures.

ANIMALS

alligator   elephant   lion   snake   llama   parrot

a. My favorite animal above is a/an _____.

b. I'm afraid of _____s.

c. I would like a/an _____ as a pet.

10. Take a dictation track 33

Use your own paper to write the dictation. Check your answers on page 87.

11. Complete the story

Use the words from the box to complete the story.

parrot	sensitive	tools	artist	feelings	upside-down

An English-Speaking Bird

NEW YORK CITY, USA "What ya doing on the phone?" N'kisi calls out to Aimee Morgana in their apartment in New York City. The question seems ordinary except N'kisi is a bird! In fact, he is one of the best users of English in the animal world.

N'kisi, an African gray **(1)** _____, can say 950 words in English. He speaks in the present, past, and future. N'kisi puts together his own words, just as a human child does. He says "flied" instead of "flew." N'kisi is also funny. He once saw another parrot hanging **(2)** _____. "You got to put this bird on the camera," N'kisi shouted.

N'kisi's owner, Aimee Morgana, is an **(3)** _____ who has strong **(4)** _____ for animals and the natural world. Her bird hears a lot of English because Aimee speaks to him six hours a day. She uses children's toys* as teaching **(5)** _____ for the bird.

Animals surprise us more every day. They are more intelligent and **(6)** _____ than scientists had thought. Professor Donald Broom of the University of Cambridge says that the more we look at animals, the smarter they appear. A conversation with N'kisi is proof**.

* toys: things for a child to play with
** proof: something that shows that an idea is true

 Talk about the stories

How are Tom (the chimp) and N'kisi (the parrot) similar? How are they different? Which one would you prefer as a pet? Why?

17

Crazy Inventions

1. Read the story

Look at the pictures on these pages.
What is the story about? Now read it.

EUROPE [1]People **invent** the craziest things! [2]An Italian company is selling **soap** that can make you smell like pizza, coffee, or even like **fresh** bread.

[3]In Britain, inventors have developed a **tiny** cell phone that can be put into your tooth. Sometime in the future, your friends will be able to **contact** you on your "phone tooth." Their voices will travel from your tooth to your ear. **Perfect**—except that you can't talk back!

[4]Some unusual clothes were invented recently. There's a $1,000 "musical **jacket**." The jacket has an MP3 player* inside, with all the **controls** sewn onto the arm. [5]"Cool shoes" keep your feet cool. The shoes have a simple machine in the back that blows cold air onto your feet as you walk. They're great for the summer **season**.

[6]There are strange inventions for your home, too. "Floating furniture" is filled with a **gas**. These chairs and sofas **float** on the ceiling until you are ready to use them—a great idea for tiny apartments! [7]And finally, there is "home snow." This small Swiss machine makes snow for your yard **in case** you don't get any natural snow for New Year's.

[8]Get ready! Who knows what other wild inventions the twenty-first century will bring?

* MP3 player: a tiny machine that plays songs

NEW WORDS

| invention *n* | soap *n* | tiny *adj* | perfect *adj* | control *n* | gas *n* | in case *conj* |
| invent *v* | fresh *adj* | contact *v* | jacket *n* | season *n* | float *v* | |

>> See Glossary on page 96. >>

2. Rate the story

How much did you like it? Mark an **✗**.

Not at All   A Lot
1   2   3   4   5

3. Check your comprehension

Match the first and second parts of the sentences.

a. Some Italian soaps make you smell ___   1. cold air onto your feet.

b. Inventors have developed ___   2. controls on the arm.

c. Cool shoes blow ___   3. snow for your yard.

d. Musical jackets have ___   4. a phone tooth.

e. Floating furniture floats ___   5. on your ceiling.

f. A Swiss machine makes ___   6. like pizza.

4. Check your vocabulary

Complete the sentences with the New Words.

a. An Italian company is selling s_ _ _ that smells like f_ _ _ _ bread.

b. Cool shoes are great for the summer se_ _ _ _.

c. All the _ _ _ _rols are sewn into the arm of the musical ja_ _ _ _.

d. _ _ _ _ _ing furniture is filled with a g_ _.

e. Home snow makes snow for you in the winter in _ _ _ _ you don't get any natural snow.

5. Listen to the story track 34

Now listen to the story two or three times. Look at the pictures below as you listen.

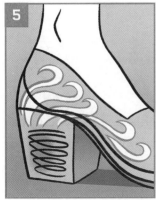   

6. Retell the story

Cover the story and look at the pictures above. Retell the story using the New Words.

7. Answer the questions

About the story...

a. Which Italian soap would you like to use?

b. Would you like a phone tooth? Why or why not?

c. How do the cool shoes work?

d. When you're not using the floating furniture, where does it stay?

About you...

e. Which of these inventions is the most useful, in your opinion?

f. Which one would you like to buy? Why?

g. Which one would you like to buy for your best friend? Why?

h. Do you have an idea for an invention? What is it?

8. Learn word partnerships

Study the partnerships below. Complete the sentences so they are true for you.

CONTACT			
contact someone	on	a cell phone	***Friends can contact you on your phone tooth.***
	by	e-mail	*I'll contact you by e-mail.*
		phone	*He contacted me by phone.*
	at	school	*I'll contact you at school.*
		work	*Contact me at work tomorrow.*
		home	*Can I contact you at home?*

a. I usually contact _____ phone.

b. _____ often contacts me at _____.

c. I plan to contact _____ by _____.

9. Learn word groups

Complete the sentences so they are true for you. Use words from the pictures.

INVENTIONS

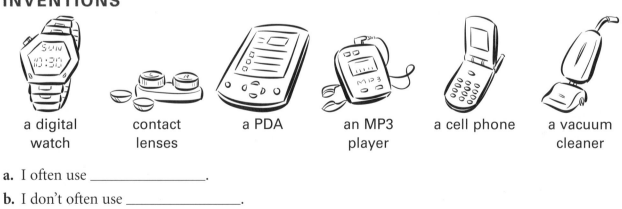

a digital watch   contact lenses   a PDA   an MP3 player   a cell phone   a vacuum cleaner

a. I often use _____.

b. I don't often use _____.

c. I think the most important invention here is _____.

10. Take a dictation track 35

Use your own paper to write the dictation. Check your answers on page 87.

11. Complete the story

Use the words from the box to complete the story.

cell phones	in case	vacuum cleaners	inventions	perfect	floats	tiny

A Floating car

LONDON, ENGLAND   Amazing new **(1)** _____ are appearing almost every day. We are getting smaller and smaller **(2)** _____ and **(3)** _____ MP3 players. There are even robot* **(4)** _____ that clean our floors without human help.

   Now there's the Aquada, a British-made car that is also a boat. You just touch a button and–like magic–it turns into a boat. The Aquada has no doors–you have to jump into it. It goes fast on the road and in the water. You can drive it either in a lake or in the ocean.

The makers say that the Aquada is a good toy, but it is also **(5)** _____ for getting to work every day in a city. You can ride on the river **(6)** _____ the roads are busy.

   The inventor, Terry Roycroft of New Zealand, has dreamed about the car for 15 years and is delighted that 100 of them have finally been made. Are you bored with your old car? Do you need a car that **(7)** _____? Then perhaps you should begin to save your money. The Aquada sells for $240,000!

_____

   * robot: a machine that can work like a person

 Talk about the stories

Which invention from the two stories do you like best? Why? Which one don't you like? Why?

18

80-Year-Old Woman Fights Rat

1. Read the story

Look at the pictures on these pages.
What is the story about? Now read it.

BRUSSELS, BELGIUM [1]What is the most frightening experience you have ever had? An 80-year-old shopper in Brussels got the **shock** of her life recently as she was shopping at a large supermarket in her **neighborhood**.

[2]The supermarket was having an annoying problem with a large **rat**. For the last month the workers had chased the rat through the store, trying their best to catch it. [3]They put out **poison**. They also put cheese* in **traps**. But neither the poison nor the traps worked. The clever rat simply ate the cheese and **kept on** avoiding the workers.

[4]Then one day the **unsuspecting** woman came into the supermarket. [5]As she picked up a package of cheese, she felt a **sharp** pain in her right hand. [6]She looked down, **horrified** to see a **nasty** rat. "It was as big as my hand and hanging on my finger," the woman told a local newspaper. The rat was trying to steal her cheese. [7]She bravely pulled the rat off with her left hand and started banging it on the floor. [8]"The animal was on the floor, knocked completely **unconscious**," said the proud woman later.

* cheese: yellow or white food made from milk

NEW WORDS

shock n	**poison** n	**unsuspecting** adj	**nasty** adj
neighborhood n	**trap** n	**sharp** adj	**unconscious** adj
rat n	**keep on** v	**horrified** adj	

>> See Glossary on page 96. >>

2. Rate the story

How much did you like it? Mark an **✗**.

Not at All   A Lot
(1)   (2)   (3)   (4)   (5)

3. Check your comprehension

Match the first and second parts of the sentences.

a. A supermarket had a problem with ___   1. steal it.

b. The workers put out traps, but ___   2. unconscious.

c. The clever animal avoided ___   3. a large rat.

d. An unsuspecting shopper picked up ___   4. a package of cheese.

e. The rat tried to ___   5. the traps and the workers.

f. The horrified woman knocked the rat ___   6. they didn't work.

4. Check your vocabulary

Complete the sentences with the New Words.

a. The supermarket workers tried to catch the _ _ _ with traps and p_ _ _ _ _, but nothing worked.

b. The nas_ _ rat _ _ _ _ on avoiding the traps.

c. When an unsus_ _ _ _ _ _ _ shopper picked up some cheese, she felt a

   sh_ _ _ pain in her hand.

d. She was ho_ _ _ _ _ _ _ to see a rat, but she bravely knocked it uncon_ _ _ _ _ _.

5. Listen to the story track 36

Now listen to the story two or three times. Look at the pictures below as you listen.

6. Retell the story

Cover the story and look at the pictures above. Retell the story using the New Words.

7. Answer the questions

About the story...

a. How did the supermarket workers try to catch the rat?

b. What did the woman feel when she picked up the package of cheese?

c. What did she see when she looked down?

d. Why did the woman feel proud of herself?

About you...

e. What was your most frightening experience?

f. Do you have an annoying problem? How can you solve it?

g. Is there a supermarket in your neighborhood? What do you buy there?

h. Do you think that poison or traps should be used when people have a problem with a small animal like a mouse or a rat? Why or why not?

8. Learn word partnerships

Study the partnerships below. Complete the sentences so they are true for you.

SHOCK			
get/have	a terrible an awful a nasty	shock	*She got a terrible shock when she saw the rat.* *I had an awful shock when I heard the news.* *He got a nasty shock at work.*
give someone a **shock**			*That dog gave me a terrible shock when it bit me.* *I gave my mother a shock when I cut my hair.*

a. I _____ a _____ shock recently when _____.

b. I gave _____ an awful shock when I _____.

9. Learn word groups

Complete the sentences so they are true for you. Use words from the picture.

A NEIGHBORHOOD

a. In my neighborhood, there is no
_____.

b. In my neighborhood, there is a
_____ and a _____.

c. My favorite place in my neighborhood is the
_____.

d. My neighborhood needs a
_____.

10. Take a dictation track 37

Use your own paper to write the dictation. Check your answers on page 87.

11. Complete the story

Use the words from the box to complete the story.

kept on	horrified	trap	got an awful shock
	neighborhood	unsuspecting	

SLEEPWALKER FIGHTS ALLIGATORS

PALM HARBOR, FLA., USA James Currens, 77, often walks in his sleep. One recent night he **(1)** _____. Still sleeping, Currens got out of bed, picked up his cane, and walked out of his house. A few minutes later, the **(2)** _____ man fell into a small lake in his **(3)** _____.

Currens woke up in several feet of water. His legs were in mud, and all around him were alligators! The animals quickly made a circle around Currens and showed their teeth. Currens was **(4)** _____! He was in a dangerous **(5)** _____. He **(6)** _____ screaming and hit the hungry animals with his cane to keep them away.

Neighbors finally heard the man's screams and called the police. When they arrived, the police turned on some bright lights, which scared the alligators. They swam away and Currens was free! It was a lucky night for him.

 Talk about the stories

Imagine that you and a partner are the 80-year-old woman and James Currens. You are meeting for the first time. Tell each other about your experiences with animals.

1. Match the words with the pictures.

___ **a.** flame   ___ **d.** painting

___ **b.** soap   ___ **e.** laboratory

___ **c.** jacket   ___ **f.** sign

1.    **2.**    **3.**

4.    **5.**    **6.**

2. Write the words in the picture.

curtains	ceiling	faucet	paint	tools	stove	rat	trap

3. Are the sentences true or false? Check (✓) the correct box.

		T	F
a.	A stone will float when you throw it into a river.	☐	☐
b.	Your chest is part of your body.	☐	☐
c.	The opposite of "sharp" is "strong".	☐	☐
d.	Poison can kill you.	☐	☐
e.	Winter and spring are seasons.	☐	☐
f.	"Cruel" is the opposite of "kind."	☐	☐
g.	A basement is at the top of a house.	☐	☐
h.	The use of computers is growing.	☐	☐

4. Circle the item that completes each sentence.

a. Many students were _____ from school yesterday.

    1. injured   2. absent   3. nasty   4. silly

b. That painting is _____.

    1. upside-down   2. unconscious   3. unsuspecting   4. horrified

c. She'll _____ you at work tomorrow.

    1. cause   2. contact   3. suggest   4. freeze

d. He was injured in a car accident last year but _____ after a few weeks.

    1. repaired   2. invented   3. trapped   4. recovered

e. I didn't like the movie. It was _____.

    1. dull   2. perfect   3. sharp   4. amazing

5. Match the definitions with the words.

a. advise ____   1. anything that is like air; for example, oxygen

b. control ____   2. to tell someone what they should do

c. by accident ____   3. the part of a machine that you move to make it work

d. shock ____   4. at the same time as something else is happening

e. meanwhile ____   5. by chance; not planned

f. gas ____   6. a very bad surprise

6. Use the words from the box to complete the sentences.

> situation   nasty   over   horrified   effects   in case   broke open
> forgiven   season   disaster   laboratories   research

a. Robbie the cat caused a _____, but he was _____.

b. After 62 hours in ice, David Blaine's stunt was _____, and his companions _____ the ice.

c. New _____ is teaching us about the amazing _____ of natural light.

d. The chimps in Quebec were test animals in _____ for many years, but now they live in a much better _____.

e. _____ your feet get hot, you can use "cool shoes" in the summer _____.

f. The 80-year-old shopper in Brussels was _____ to see a _____ rat hanging on her finger.

7. Use the words from the box to complete the story.

> pets   would rather   tiny   amazing
> sensitive   perfect

Dog Cafe

ILSAN, KOREA   An **(1)** _____ new cafe has opened in Korea. It is called the Dog Cafe. People can borrow dogs there. Customers who have no **(2)** _____ at home can now enjoy a meal or a cup of coffee with a dog at their side.

You can eat while your dog lies at your feet. Or, if you **(3)** _____ watch the dog eat too, you can buy him a delicious meal. You can even pay for your pet to get a bath. There are 25 different kinds of dogs at the cafe— some **(4)** _____, some large. "The dogs are completely safe," says

Gwang-ho Jeong, the owner of the cafe. "I trained them all myself. They're even **(5)** _____ for little children."

Mr. Jeong is a **(6)** _____ man who has loved dogs since he was a child. "It was natural for me to start a business where I can be with dogs," he says.

8. Check (✓) yes or no.

	Yes	No			Yes	No
a. I have a lot of energy.	☐	☐	**f.** I occasionally paint.		☐	☐
b. I'm a sensitive person.	☐	☐	**g.** I have a pet.		☐	☐
c. My favorite season is winter.	☐	☐	**h.** I enjoy working with tools.		☐	☐
d. I have a very good mind.	☐	☐	**i.** I often do research on the Internet.		☐	☐
e. I eat a lot of fresh fruit.	☐	☐	**j.** I like electric light better than natural.		☐	☐

9. Complete the sentences so they are true for you.

a. _____ encourages me to _____.

b. _____ is a famous artist in my country.

c. I think _____ is amazing because _____.

d. I often contact _____ by _____.

e. I will keep on _____ for many more years.

f. I love fresh _____.

g. There is _____ in my neighborhood.

h. I have strong feelings about _____.

10. Fill in the chart with names of classmates. Try to write a different name in each blank. Walk around the room and ask questions such as:

Were you injured recently?
Do you think TV is dull?

The winner is the first person to fill in seven blanks.

FIND SOMEONE WHO…

a. was injured recently. _____

b. thinks TV is dull. _____

c. owns a lot of tools. _____

d. likes to paint. _____

e. has two or more pets. _____

f. wants to keep on studying English. _____

g. has a black jacket. _____

h. is occasionally absent from school. _____

i. can repair a bike or a car. _____

j. likes to do research. _____

Unit 1

Would you like to go sightseeing in space? Dennis Tito loved the experience. After training for six months, he took a trip to the international space station. He said it was unbelievable to see the Earth from above. He also loved being weightless and dancing with his Russian companions.

Unit 2

Sabriye believes that all children have special gifts. The children and teenagers in her school have lost their sight, but they can do many things. They read in the dark and go climbing and rafting. Sabriye and her students have made a decision to live life fully!

Unit 3

Many Amish live simply, without electricity or telephones. Some avoid cars and ride only in carriages. The women often bake their own bread and sew their own dresses. The Amish want to keep their old customs, and they consider new ideas carefully.

Unit 4

Lee is a famous moviemaker today, but he had some tough years. He was a shy child who had many responsibilities at home. He didn't get good grades in school. When Lee failed the college entrance test, his family was disappointed. However, Lee's parents are very proud of him now.

Unit 5

Sharon and Jack are delighted to live in a house made of trash. The couple collected most of the building materials themselves. The walls are made of old tires, cans, bottles, mud, and dirt. An earthquake cannot damage the walls since they are extremely strong.

Unit 6

Jens was fortunate to survive a whole night in the ocean. Strong, rough waves pulled him away from the beach. Jens became exhausted and weak, but he held on to his surfboard. The sun began to rise just as he couldn't hold on any longer.

Unit 7

Have you found your dream job? Annie Lever has. She is a professional dog walker. At present, she earns $25.00 a day for each dog. She enjoys the freedom of being her own boss.

According to Wally Amos, young people should always keep their eyes open for a dream job and not miss any opportunity.

Unit 8

The Okinawans have excellent eating habits. They are regular eaters of fish and tofu, and they eat at least seven fruits and vegetables a day. They also eat light meals. As a result, their hearts, bones, and muscles stay strong and healthy.

Unit 9

Are the Harry Potter novels on your shelf? The boy is one of the most famous characters in the world. His creator, J.K. Rowling, grew up in England, playing in fields full of magic. Harry appeared in her head all at once in 1990 while she was sitting on a train.

Unit 10

Holidays are especially hard for single people. Two German women have developed a new wallpaper for them. It shows life-size photos of people doing routine things. These paper friends always behave well. They won't annoy you by leaving dirty dishes on your coffee table.

Unit 11

Advertising has reached a new level. An agency is hiring students to become human billboards. Students like Stuart Charles think the job is fun. He liked earning cash while sitting with friends at local clubs and cafes. Everyone had an opinion about the ad on his forehead.

Unit 12

When Ji Haye went to Paris, she was eager to make her fortune. She worked under famous designers during the day but drew her own designs at night. Finally, she was invited to a fashion show. She did all the details herself, pushing and pulling a needle and thread until her arms were swollen.

Unit 13

Robbie the cat turned on an upstairs faucet by accident. Water ran all the way down to the basement. When the German couple ran down to save their things, flames jumped from the stove to the rest of the kitchen. Everything in the kitchen was destroyed—the stove, the cabinets, and the refrigerator. The couple will repair the damage.

Unit 14

Blaine was trapped in a block of ice for three days. His fans held up signs encouraging him to go on. After 62 hours, Blaine couldn't take it any longer. He felt like he had lost his mind. Someone broke open the ice and Blaine went to the hospital, where he recovered.

Unit 15

Open up your curtains, and put skylights in your home! New research suggests that the use of sunlight rather than electric light is good for you. Workers are absent less often in sunny offices, and they work harder. Sunlight gives you energy, and Dr. Kime advises us to get plenty of it!

Unit 16

Binky had a cruel life in a laboratory. Now he is in a much better situation and has become an artist. Binky would rather paint with his fingers than with a brush. You can really see his feelings in his strong and sensitive paintings.

Unit 17

People invent wonderful things. There are tiny MP3 players and cell phones. There are also some crazy inventions. There is soap that makes you smell like fresh bread, furniture that floats, and cool shoes for the summer season. A Swiss machine makes snow in case you don't get any natural snow.

Unit 18

A shopper recently got a terrible shock at her neighborhood supermarket. When the woman picked up some cheese, she felt a sharp pain in her hand. She was horrified to see a nasty rat on her finger. The brave woman knocked it unconscious.

Glossary

Unit 1

experience *n* something that has happened to you

space *n* the place far away from the world, where all the planets and stars are

international *adj* between different countries

train *v* to make yourself ready for something

unbelievable *adj* very surprising or unusual

Earth *n* our world; the planet we live on

completely *adv* in every way; fully

weightless *adj* without any heaviness

companion *n* a person who is with another person; a friend

enthusiastic *adj* liking something very much

grow up *v* to change from a child to an adult

sightseeing *n* visiting interesting places

trip *n* a short journey to a place

Unit 2

blind *adj* not able to see

sight *n* the power to see

decision *n* a choice that you make after thinking

teenager *n* a person who is between the ages of 13 and 19

college *n* a place where people go to study after high school

history *n* all the things that happened in the past

guide *n* a person who shows people where to go

cliff *n* the straight side of a high hill or mountain

distant *adj* far away

desperate *adj* without hope; ready to do anything to get what you want

attempt *v* to try

believe *v* to feel sure that something is true

gift *n* something you can do well or easily; natural ability

Unit 3

countryside *n* land with farms and forests that is away from towns

state *n* a part of a country

carriage *n* a kind of car that is pulled by horses

electricity *n* the power that comes through wires and makes heat, light, and other things work

simply *adv* in a plain, basic way

custom *n* something that a group of people usually does

avoid *v* to stay away from something or someone

basket *n* a container used to carry or hold things

sew *v* to make clothes by hand or with a machine

bake *v* to cook foods like bread, cakes, and cookies

frozen *adj* unchanging

consider *v* to think carefully about something

simple *adj* without a lot of different parts or extra things; plain

Unit 4

tiger *n* a wild animal like a big cat; it is yellow and black

shy *adj* afraid to talk to people you do not know

principal *n* a person who is the head of a school

responsibility *n* something that you must do

expect *v* to think that someone will do something

however *conj* but

test *n* a group of questions which measures how much someone knows

disappointed *adj* sad because what you wanted did not happen

tough *adj* difficult

competition *n* a game or test that people try to win

proud *adj* pleased about something that you or others have done

forever *adv* for all time

city *n* a big, important town

solve *v* to find the answer to a problem

collect *v* to take things from different places and put them together

building material *n* what you use for building a house, like wood or stone

tire *n* the round, black part of a car wheel

dirt *n* black stuff from the ground

consist of *v* to be made of something

mud *n* soft, wet dirt

extremely *adv* very

since *conj* because

earthquake *n* a sudden, strong shaking of the ground

couple *n* two people who are married

bury *v* to put something under the ground

delighted *adj* very pleased or happy

ocean *n* a very big sea

rough *adj* not calm or gentle

wave *n* one of the lines of water that move across the top of the sea

shore *n* the land next to the sea or ocean

hold on *v* to keep something in your hand

exhausted *adj* very tired

weak *adj* not strong

drown *v* to die underwater because you cannot swim

horrible *adj* very bad; scary

whole *adj* all

any longer *adv* no more

rise *v* to go up

fortunate *adj* lucky

survive *v* to continue to live after a difficult or dangerous time

Unit 7

according to *prep* as someone or something says

mention *v* to speak a little about something

professor *n* a teacher at a university

professional *adj* doing something as a job for money

earn *v* to get money by working

freedom *n* being free

tester *n* a person who tries something to see if it works well

hobby *n* something that you like doing when you are not working

at present *adv* now

though *adv* however

delicious *adj* very good to eat

boss *n* the person at work who tells the other workers what to do

opportunity *n* a time when you can do something that you want to do; a chance

Unit 8

imagine *v* to make a picture of something in your head

rare *adj* if something is rare, you do not find or see it often

else *adv* different; other

habit *n* something that you do very often

at least *adv* not less than

be fond of *v* to like something or someone a lot

regular *adj* happening again and again

light *adj* not heavy

as a result *adv* because of something

bone *n* one of the hard white parts inside the body

rush *v* to do something quickly

tie *n* something that holds people together

heart attack *n* a sudden, dangerous illness when your heart stops working

Unit 9

character *n* a person in a book or film

creator *n* a person who makes something new

surrounding *adj* being all around something

magic *n* something that makes strange or impossible things happen

misfortune *n* something bad that happens; bad luck

marriage *n* the time when two people are husband and wife

break up *v* to end a relationship such as a marriage

depressed *adj* very unhappy

all at once *adv* suddenly

cafe *n* a place where you can have a drink and something small to eat

receive *v* to get something from someone

shelf *n* a long, flat piece of wood on a wall, where things like books can stand

Unit 10

especially *adv* more than usual

particularly *adv* especially; more than others

develop *v* to work on something and make it more complete

life-size *adj* as big as a real person or thing

routine *adj* regular; usual; not special

sofa *n* a long soft seat for more than one person

hang *v* to attach from above; put on a wall

apartment *n* a group of rooms for living in, in a larger building

advantage *n* something that helps you or is useful

behave *v* to act in a particular way with other people

annoy *v* to make someone a little angry

frequently *adv* often

apart *adv* away from each other

copy *n* a thing that is made to look the same as something else

Unit 11

advertisement *n* information that tells you to buy something

ugly *adj* not beautiful

level *n* a particular standard or quantity

human *adj* of or like people, not animals

hire *v* to pay someone to do a job for you

forehead *n* the part of your face above your eyes

attractive *adj* nice to look at; pleasing; not ugly

local *adj* of a place near you

club *n* a place where young people meet at night to listen to music

opinion *n* what you think about something

cash *n* money

later on *adv* at a later time

Unit 12

confused *adj* not able to think clearly

uncertain *adj* not sure

eager *adj* wanting to do something very much

fortune *n* success; good luck; a lot of money

designer *n* a person who draws things to show how something will be made

give up *v* to stop trying

draw *v* to make a picture with a pencil

design *n* a drawing that shows how to make something

prepare *v* to get something ready

detail *n* one of the very small parts that make the whole of something

needle *n* a small thin piece of metal with a hole that you use to make clothes

material *n* something like cotton that you use for making clothes

traditional *adj* following or using customs that have not changed for a long time

pet *n* an animal that you keep in your home

disaster *n* something very bad that happens and that may hurt a lot of people

by accident *adv* by chance; not planned

faucet *n* a thing that you turn in your bathroom or kitchen to make water come out

ceiling *n* the part of a room over your head

basement *n* the part of a building that is under the ground

meanwhile *adv* at the same time as something else is happening

stove *n* the thing that you use in a kitchen for cooking food

flame *n* a hot, bright piece of fire

injure *v* to hurt

repair *v* to fix; to make something that is broken good again

forgive *v* to stop being angry at someone for a bad thing that he or she did

block *n* a big, heavy piece of something, with flat sides

mind *n* the part of you that thinks and remembers

trap *v* to keep someone in a place that he or she cannot escape from

separate *v* to keep people or things away from each other

chest *n* the front part of your body below your shoulders and above your stomach

freeze *v* to become very cold and hard, like ice

encourage *v* to give someone hope or help so that they can do something

sign *n* a thing with writing or a picture on it that tells you something

break open *v* to make something go into pieces by hitting it

over *adv* finished

recover *v* to get well again after you have been sick

dull *adj* not interesting or exciting

occasionally *adv* sometimes, but not often

silly *adj* stupid; not clever or smart

Unit 15

amazing *adj* very surprising

research *n* a careful studying of something to find out more about it

effect *n* a change that happens because of something

light *n* light helps people see things; it comes from the sun, fire, and electricity

suggest *v* to say what you think should or will happen

absent *adj* not there; away

use *n* what you can do with something

electric *adj* using electricity to make something work

advise *v* to tell someone what you think they should do

energy *n* the ability to do many things without getting tired

cause *v* to make something happen

curtain *n* a piece of material that covers a window

Unit 16

paint *v* to make a picture with wet colors

painting *n* a picture that you make with wet colors

feeling *n* something that you feel inside yourself or in your heart, like happiness

would rather *v* to prefer

artist *n* a person who paints or draws pictures

sensitive *adj* careful about your own and other people's feelings

cruel *adj* unkind or hurtful

laboratory *n* a special room where scientists work

situation *n* the things that are happening at a certain place or time

tool *n* a thing that you use to do a special job

upside-down *adv* with the top part at the bottom

paint *n* wet colors that you use to make a picture

Unit 17

invention *n* a thing that someone has made for the first time

invent *v* to make or think of something new

soap *n* something that you use with water for washing or cleaning

fresh *adj* made a short time ago

tiny *adj* very small

contact *v* to talk to someone by phone, e-mail, etc.

perfect *adj* very good, with nothing wrong

jacket *n* a short coat

control *n* the part of a machine that you move to make it work

season *n* a part of the year like summer or winter

gas *n* anything that is like air; for example, oxygen

float *v* to move slowly in the air

in case *conj* because something might happen

Unit 18

shock *n* a very bad surprise

neighborhood *n* a part of a town or city

rat *n* an animal with a long tail, like a big mouse

poison *n* something that can kill you if you eat or drink it

trap *n* a thing that you use for catching animals

keep on *v* to do something many times

unsuspecting *adj* not thinking that something will happen

sharp *adj* strong and sudden

horrified *adj* surprised and scared

nasty *adj* bad; not nice

unconscious *adj* in a kind of sleep; not knowing what is happening

Index

A

absent *adj* 66
according to *prep* 30, 33, 66
advantage *n* 42, 45
advertisement *n* 46, 49
advise *v* 66, 69
all at once *adv* 38, 41
amazing *adj* 66, 69, 77
annoy *v* 42
any longer *adv* 22
apart *adv* 42
apartment *n* 42, 45, 73, 74
artist *n* 70, 73
as a result *adv* 34, 37, 66
at least *adv* 34
at present *adv* 30, 33
attempt *v* 6
attractive *adj* 46
avoid *v* 10, 13, 34, 78

B

bake *v* 10, 13
basement *n* 58
basket *n* 10
be fond of *v* 34, 37
behave *v* 42, 45
believe *v* 6, 9, 65
blind *adj* 6, 9
block *n* 62, 65
bone *n* 34, 37
boss *n* 30, 33
break open *v* 62
break up *v* 38
building material *n* 18
bury *v* 18, 62
by accident *adv* 58

C

cafe *n* 38, 46
carriage *n* 10, 13
cash *n* 46, 49
cause *v* 66, 69
ceiling *n* 58, 61, 74
character *n* 38, 41
chest *n* 62
city *n* 18, 21, 70, 77
cliff *n* 6, 50
club *n* 46
collect *v* 18, 21
college *n* 6, 14, 46
companion *n* 2, 42, 45, 62
competition *n* 14, 17, 49
completely *adv* 2, 5, 10, 58, 78
confused *adj* 50, 65
consider *v* 10
consist of *v* 18
contact *v* 74
control *n* 74
copy *n* 42
countryside *n* 10
couple *n* 18, 42, 58
creator *n* 38, 41, 42
cruel *adj* 70
curtain *n* 66
custom *n* 10, 13

D

decision *n* 6
delicious *adj* 30
delighted *adj* 18, 21, 77
depressed *adj* 38, 41
design *n* 50, 53
designer *n* 50

desperate *adj* 6, 9, 14
detail *n* 50, 53
develop *v* 42, 45, 74
dirt *n* 18
disappointed *adj* 14
disaster *n* 58, 61
distant *adj* 6, 9, 22
draw *v* 41, 50
drown *v* 22
dull *adj* 62

E

eager *adj* 50, 53
earn *v* 30, 33, 46
Earth *n* 2, 66
earthquake *n* 18
effect *n* 66, 69
electric *adj* 66
electricity *n* 10, 13, 18, 66
else *adv* 34
encourage *v* 62, 65
energy *n* 66
enthusiastic *adj* 2
especially *adv* 42
exhausted *adj* 22, 25
expect *v* 14, 17
experience *n* 2, 78
extremely *adv* 18, 21, 34, 38

F

faucet *n* 58
feeling *n* 70, 73
flame *n* 58, 61
float *v* 74, 77
forehead *n* 46
forever *adv* 14, 17

shore *n* 22, 25, 65

shy *adj* 14

sight *n* 6, 9

sightseeing *n* 2

sign *n* 62

silly *adj* 62, 69

simple *adj* 10, 13, 46, 74

simply *adv* 10

since *conj* 18, 70

situation *n* 70

soap *n* 74

sofa *n* 42, 45, 74

solve *v* 18, 21, 42

space *n* 2, 5

state *n* 10

stove *n* 58

suggest *v* 66, 69

surrounding *adj* 38

survive *v* 22, 25

T

teenager *n* 6, 9, 30, 50

test *n* 14, 62, 66

tester *n* 30

though *adv* 30, 33

tie *n* 34

tiger *n* 14

tiny *adj* 74, 77

tire *n* 18

tool *n* 70, 73

tough *adj* 14

traditional *adj* 50, 53

train *v* 2, 5

trap *n* 78, 81

trap *v* 62

trip *n* 2, 5, 41

U

ugly *adj* 46, 49

unbelievable *adj* 2, 5

uncertain *adj* 50

unconscious *adj* 78

unsuspecting *adj* 78, 81

upside-down *adv* 70, 73

use *n* 66

W

wave *n* 22, 25

weak *adj* 22, 25, 70

weightless *adj* 2

whole *adj* 22, 25, 50, 58, 61, 70

would rather *v* 70